WINDS OF CHANGE
in the
CHRISTIAN MISSION

WINDS OF CHANGE
in the
CHRISTIAN MISSION

by

J. HERBERT KANE

MOODY PRESS

CHICAGO

1973

ISBN: 0-8024-9561-3

Second Printing, 1973

Printed in the United States of America

To

WINNIE,

for forty years my faithful companion

in the service of Christ

CONTENTS

FOREWORD

"STUDENTS, I want you to know that missions have ten years left in Africa! If we don't get the job done in that time, it will be too late."

The missionary leader who made that statement twenty-five years ago stands out clearly in my mind to this day. And he was not alone in his prophecies. As college students in the immediate post-World War II era, we were barraged with such prophecies.

A professor in my college made the statement that no one in my class would ever get to the mission field. Two and a half decades later hundreds who were students at that time are still serving God effectively around the world, including Africa.

Today, after some years overseas in spite of prophecies to the contrary, I am once again involved in the student world. And, once again, the question is being raised with increasing frequency about the future of the world mission of the church. Is the missionary enterprise doomed? Is the task of the foreign missionary over? Aren't we in a new era?

J. Herbert Kane comes to grips with this on the first page of his book. "Time and again in recent years we have been warned that the missionary movement is rapidly coming to an end. . . . So, we are told, missions are at the crossroads." He meets this charge head on and states, "Missions are indeed at the crossroads, but that should not unduly disturb us. Missions have always been at the crossroads. That is where they began. That is where they belong."

Thus the tone for this book is set. The author is neither a pessimistic crier of doom nor a sentimental optimist. Rather Dr. Kane is a realist. He is willing to face the facts as they are. He discusses calmly the poor image that the missionary has today. He faces without panic the paucity of candidates. He analyzes the reasons for missionary dropouts. He draws a picture of the new

9

missionary for the new day. He compares the merits and problems of the Peace Corps, nonprofessional missions, and the short-term assignment with the traditional missionary program of the church.

The author does not hide from the problems which beset the mission of the church nor the potential pitfalls of the future. In discussing closed doors he looks at the issue both positively and negatively. He does not pretend that such problems don't exist. But neither does he ring down the curtain on missions just because of some problems.

If there is one thing that young people want today it is honesty. They will find it in this book. Dr. Kane speaks from years of experience overseas and years of mingling with students as a professor of missions in this country. And he speaks honestly. In so doing he gives a realistic portrayal of what the church faces in the latter part of the twentieth century in seeking to be faithful to the unfulfilled commission given by Jesus Christ.

For those who want to know what the problems are, this book will tell them. And for those who want to announce the arrival of doomsday for missions, this book will be a good antidote. The worldwide responsibility of the church will end when Jesus Christ returns. Until that day we need more realists such as J. Herbert Kane to keep our task in focus.

DAVID M. HOWARD
Missions Director
Inter-Varsity Christian Fellowship

PREFACE

WE ARE LIVING in a new day with all kinds of exciting opportunities for Christian witness at home and overseas. In fact the options are so numerous that many members of the younger generation are confused. Shall I follow a "secular calling" or shall I prepare for "Christian service"? Shall I serve the Lord in the asphalt jungles of the inner city, in the green pastures of modern suburbia, or in some far-off foreign land? If I become a missionary should I sign up for life, or should I settle for a short term? If I take the pains to go overseas, should I join a mission or the Peace Corps, or should I go it alone? The options are legion.

Along with the options comes an equal number of questions. If doors are closing here and there, isn't the missionary era just about over? If the indigenous church is an established fact, what's left for me to do? If missionaries are still needed, are they still wanted? If I become a missionary, will I make the grade? What about all those dropouts we hear about? Must I be a missionary? Can't I serve the Lord in the Peace Corps? If I join a mission, will they put me in a straitjacket? Would I have greater freedom and more opportunities as a nonprofessional missionary? Can't I go just as I am without any special training?

These and many other questions are flooding the minds of Christian youth today. They are legitimate questions and demand honest answers.

This book is a modest attempt to answer some of these questions.

1

MISSIONS AT THE CROSSROADS

TIME AND AGAIN in recent years we have been warned that the missionary movement is rapidly coming to an end. Almost everywhere Christianity has been identified with colonialism; and, now that the colonial system has broken up, the assumption is that the missionary is on the way out.

On every hand the prophets of doom are predicting the early demise of the most magnificent, most magnanimous enterprise the world has ever seen. And they don't have to look far for documentation. In Asia the ancient religions of the East are on the march and giving the missionary a run for his money. In Africa, where some forty nations have come to birth since 1960, the scene is marked by civil wars, military coups, and political assassinations. In Latin America, where governments rise and fall almost with the barometer, military dictators are putting up a last-ditch fight against what Adlai Stevenson called "a revolution of rising expectations." All the while, "Yankee Go Home" is scribbled across the billboards of the world. So, we are told, missions are at the crossroads.

The Vasco-da-Gama era ended abruptly with World War II. Since that time we have witnessed unprecedented changes in the political configuration of the world. First in Asia and later in Africa, the colonial countries threw off their shackles and joined the United Nations as sovereign independent states. Thus colonialism, the most powerful force in the nineteenth century, has given way to nationalism, by far the greatest force in the twentieth century.

All of this has enormous significance for the missionary movement of our day. For better or worse, the missionary movement was part and parcel of the vast colonial system which the West imposed by force on the East. The merchants, the missionaries, and the diplomats all had a stake in the empire building of the nineteenth century. Nowhere was this more clearly seen than in China, which was opened to Western influence by the treaties which followed the Opium War in 1842. The merchants with their opium and the missionaries with their Bibles arrived at the same time and demanded the same protection. American missionaries were on board the *Morrison* when it sailed into Japan's Yedo Bay in 1837, sixteen years before Commodore Perry sailed into Tokyo Bay. In Africa it was the missionaries who called for outright annexation to halt the iniquitous slave trade which was decimating the population. In the South Pacific islands, the missionaries acted as advisors to the viceroys and governors, even assisting in drawing up the laws.

It was customary for the missionaries, when they got into trouble, to appeal to their consuls for help. The Western powers were looking for an excuse to encroach on the sovereignty of the Afro-Asian countries. Consequently they were only too glad to come to the aid of the beleaguered missionaries when their property was destroyed or their lives threatened. The violent death of a missionary sometimes became the occasion for his government to make outrageous demands on the host country. In one or two instances whole provinces were wrested from a weak power in compensation for the death of a missionary. Hence there developed an unholy alliance between the gospel and the gunboat.

Now all this has changed. Except for a few pockets of colonialism here and there, the countries of Africa and Asia are masters in their own house. This is right and proper, but it poses serious problems for the Christian mission.

Now that these countries are independent, their governments insist on ordering their foreign policy as well as their domestic affairs to suit themselves. They have shown that they don't *have* to vote with us in the United Nations. During the Cold War they maintained the right to line up with the East or the West or to remain unaligned. Moreover, they have every right to exclude or expel from their domain any person they deem undesirable—including the missionary. This means that visas may be harder to get. Quotas for expatriates may be established. Some countries, such as Burma, have excluded all foreigners. Others, such as

Syria, have excluded all missionaries. Others, such as Afghanistan, accept only nonprofessional missionaries. Others, such as Malaysia and the Philippines, have been known to exclude the specialist but receive the general missionary. The pattern is by no means uniform. Some countries will allow the missionaries to remain for a certain number of years, after which their visas will not be renewed. Malaysia is an example of this. Other countries, such as Thailand, oblige the missionaries without permanent visas to leave the country every ten weeks. After a short sojourn in a neighboring country where they renew their visas, they return to Thailand. Such an arrangement is very costly in time and money, to say nothing of convenience and continuity.

The coming of independence has hurt the missions financially. Some countries impose a staggering duty on certain imports, including relief and medical supplies. Others refuse to allow certain "luxury" items to enter the country. Property taxes and personal income taxes have added to the financial burden of both the mission and the missionary.

Once the victims of racial discrimination, the new nations are extremely suspicious of anything that smacks of segregation. For many years it has been the practice of the mission boards to operate their own private schools for the children of missionaries. Some governments have charged these missions with discrimination and demanded that the schools be thrown open to all children. If nationals are admitted, drastic changes in the curriculum would become necessary. Such changes would almost certainly undermine the original purpose of the school.

In colonial days medical personnel were welcomed with open arms and went to work immediately upon their arrival. This too has changed. In many countries foreign medical personnel, regardless of their academic background or professional competence, are required to take a government-sponsored examination. Some doctors, unable to pass these examinations given in the vernacular language, are obliged to function as general missionaries.

With the rise of nationalism and the coming of independence there has been a marked resurgence in the great ethnic religions of Asia. In colonial times the indigenous cultures were plowed under. Now they are being revived and refurbished. Included in these cultures are the religions of the East. Forty or fifty years ago many missionaries, including some experts, were of the opinion that these religions were on their way out. Nobody talks that way today. It is true, of course, that intellectuals the world over tend to be disenchanted with religion; but it would be a grave mistake to suggest that the non-Christian religions are losing their grip on the people as a whole.

Hinduism is far from dying out in India. Buddhism is on the march in Southeast Asia. State Shinto in Japan was disestablished by General MacArthur; but there is reason to believe that it is on the way back. Nichiren Buddhism, aggressively propagated by Soka Gakkai, is definitely on the march, not only in Japan but overseas as well. The progress of Islam may have been slowed in Africa, but it remains a viable force in the Middle East.

Throughout most of Asia there is an attempt not only to rejuvenate the indigenous religions but also to equate them with patriotism. To be a Christian is to be a second-class citizen in the thinking of the people, if not in the eyes of the law. To be a patriotic member of society in Thailand, one must be a Buddhist. The same is true in Burma and in Sri Lanka. To be a good Indian, one should really be a Hindu. In Pakistan it pays to be a Muslim.

The coming of independence has had a direct bearing on certain phases of missionary work. Take education, for example. Wherever missionaries have gone, they have operated schools not only for the children of their own converts but for others as well. For many decades in Black Africa the missions were the sole purveyor of education. Today there is scarcely an African leader in any walk of life that did not receive at least part of his education in a mission school, Protestant or Catholic.

One of the first things the new governments do when they come to power is to nationalize all private schools. This is not hard to understand. Education is too potent an instrument for the molding of the national character to be left in the hands of foreigners, no matter how high-minded they may be. Hence one government after another has taken over the mission schools, beginning at the elementary level and proceeding step-by-step to the secondary and tertiary levels.

And what about medical work? Here too the missions were pioneers. For many decades they provided the lion's share of all medical facilities and services. China is said to have been opened "at the point of the lancet." In Korea, Thailand, and elsewhere medical missions helped pave the way for evangelistic missions. In the Muslim world, schools and hospitals were the only institutions the missionaries were permitted to establish. In Africa, practically all medical services were provided by the missions. Only in Japan did medical missions make a minor contribution.

Here, too, we note a change. Most of the independent countries of the Third World have opted for a socialist form of government. This means, among other things, socialized medicine. With tax money at their disposal these governments are able to provide wider and better medical services than the missions. New hospitals with modern equipment are springing up everywhere. One by one mission hospitals are passing under government control. Even the hospitals that remain under mission control are becoming increasingly difficult to operate efficiently. Government-imposed standards, bureaucratic red tape, the keeping of copious records, and the filing of endless reports tax the time and patience of missionary doctors as well as administrators.

The most vexing of all problems is church-mission tension. The spirit of nationalism, running very strong in the Third World, has infected the churches. They have suddenly come of age and are demanding full autonomy. Some churches, of course, received their independence years ago before even the governments got theirs. However, this was the exception, not the rule. Most missions dragged their feet, and when political independence came, neither they nor the churches were ready for it. Consequently tensions developed which have marred church-mission relations during the past decade. This is a problem that must be solved if the missions are to survive the decade of the seventies.

The situation differs from continent to continent, and even from country to country. Where missions have been progressive and churches have been patient, the prevailing climate is still harmonious. Alas! not all missions are progressive; not all churches are patient. And when an impatient church confronts a reactionary mission the sparks are bound to fly.

In some cases the relationship between church and mission is a happy one. Some churches are willing to settle for any kind of partnership that recognizes their independence and promises to promote their welfare. Other churches are demanding outright autonomy, including full control over mission subsidies as well as foreign personnel. These churches are reaching for the sky, whereas the missions don't want to go much above the horizon. The stickiest of all problems is the use of foreign funds. This raises a number of questions.

Can the churches on the mission field be truly self-governing if they are not fully self-supporting? Is it realistic to expect these churches, at this stage in their development, to assume full responsibility for all departments of the work? If foreign funds are used, will there be any strings attached? Will the churches be expected to account to the missions for all foreign funds received and disbursed? Finally, will the supporting churches in the homeland be as keen to subsidize the overseas churches as they have been to support their own foreign missions?

With these and many other problems unsolved, little wonder that we are being told that missions are at the crossroads.

What shall we say to these things? Our reply is: if history is anything to go by, the present situation vis-à-vis the church universal is not without precedent. Missions are indeed at the crossroads, but that should not unduly disturb us. Missions have always been at the crossroads. That is where they began. That is where they belong.

Mao Tse-tung said, on one occasion, that a revolution is not an invitation to a tea party. The same can be said of the missionary enterprise. Missionary work has always been difficult, dangerous, and discouraging. The mission field is no place for the weak, the weary, the fainthearted, or the double-minded. If the glorious missionary enterprise of our day is to remain true to its own genius and realize its high destiny, it must continue to operate within the context of world history, however turbulent it might become.

We do well to remember that the Christian mission is God's mission, not ours. The mandate given to us by our Lord in the Great Commission is to continue "to the end of the world" (Mt 28:20). The early church expected the end of the world to occur in their time, but two thousand years have come and gone and the church is still here. When Jesus Christ gave His apostles their marching orders, He pulled no punches; He painted no rosy pictures; He promised neither immediate victory nor universal success. Rather He spoke of opposition and persecution. He warned them that they would be hated of all men. The worldwide missionary enterprise was to be fraught with all kinds of difficulties and dangers. The messengers of the cross would be hunted and hounded from pillar to post. They would be scourged by the Jews and flogged by the Romans. Indeed, some of them would lay down their lives for the sake of the gospel.

But the mandate would never be rescinded or the mission aborted. If the disciples were persecuted in one city, they were not to throw in the towel. They were to move on to the next city. Neither the mischief of men nor the machinations of the devil were to deter them. They were taught to believe that they were engaged in a holy war with an implacable foe. Casualties would occur and reverses come; but they were to press on in full confidence that the Captain of their salvation would be with them to the end of the age. Many battles would be lost, but the war would be won. On that point there was no doubt.

We do well to bear this in mind when the modern prophets of doom are sounding the death knell of the Christian mission. To be sure, we are living in troublous times and no one knows what tomorrow will bring; but we do know that Jesus Christ is not only the Head of the church; He is also the Lord of history. Dictators come and go; kingdoms rise and fall; civilizations wax and wane; but the worldwide mission of the church will continue to the end of the age.

If worst comes to worst and all Western missionaries become persona non grata in the Third World, African and Asian missionaries will be available to step into the breach. If all expatriate missionaries, East and West, are excluded from a given country, there will still be the national church to carry on. If the church is forced to go underground, there will still remain the Spirit of God, who dwells not in temples made with hands but in the hearts of His people. Let us never underestimate His power. It is one thing to outlaw the institutional church; it is quite another to get rid of Almighty God. Heaven is His throne and earth is His footstool. It is impossible to banish Him from any part of His domain.

2

WHAT HAPPENED TO THE HALO?

WHEN I CAME to Trinity Evangelical Divinity School in 1967, the first question put to me by a group of concerned students was: What can be done to enhance the missionary image? It is a question that is being asked with increasing frequency and urgency, especially by the younger generation. It is an honest question which demands an honest answer. What has happened to the halo?

The Christian missionary has always had his critics. Ever since Festus declared that Paul was beside himself, the emissaries of the cross have been regarded by the world as fools and fanatics. Paul himself acknowledged that he and his fellow apostles were considered to be the scum of the earth. In our own day Nathaniel Peffer, writing of the missionary movement in China in his book, *The Far East*, says:

> There was fundamentally something unhealthy and incongruous in the whole missionary idea. . . . Only men of inner limitation, both intellectually and spiritually, can gratuitously thrust their beliefs on others on the assumption that they alone have the truth.[1]

Through the centuries the church continued to defend and support its missionaries in spite of all the opposition. Now, for the first time, in the twentieth century, the criticism is coming from within the church. The old-timers, the prayer warriors, the missionary-minded folks, are still staunch supporters of the enterprise; but the younger generation, especially college students, are disenchanted with the whole business. Missionary meetings in

1. Nathaniel Peffer, *The Far East: A Modern History* (Ann Arbor, Mich.: U. of M. Press, 1968).

the local church are not well attended; and the annual missionary conference, at least in its traditional form, is on the way out. Only on Sunday morning is the missionary speaker likely to have a large audience; but on that occasion the large attendance is prompted by custom rather than interest.

The hardest place of all to get a sympathetic hearing is in the college chapel. Indeed, some Christian colleges no longer invite missionaries to speak in chapel. The Bible schools continue the practice, but with diminishing response on the part of the student body. So widespread is the antipathy to missionary speakers that some missionaries actually prefer not to appear before a student group. It should be noted, of course, that today's students are critical about many things, the missionary being but one of them. Anybody who represents the establishment is suspect; and if he happens to be on the wrong side of thirty, it's just too bad. Alas, most missionaries are wrong on both counts! For a bald-headed, fifty-year-old missionary to establish rapport with the college community is a tall order. To hold their attention as a speaker, he must be knowledgeable but not pedantic, eloquent but not rhetorical, self-confident but not dogmatic. To gain their respect as a person, he must be devout but not pious, outgoing but not effusive, sincere but not sanctimonius. Above all, he must not be a milquetoast. The sin of all sins is to be corny.

For many years the missionary's personal appearance was a stumbling block. This was especially true of women missionaries. Hair style, length of dress, absence of makeup, shabby clothes all made the missionary stick out like a sore thumb. In recent years we haven't heard so much criticism along these lines, principally because weird hair styles and shabby clothes are "in," especially with the younger set. The problem today is that missionaries are too neat in their appearance!

Missionaries have been criticized for being poor speakers—long on words and short on ideas. According to the critics, missionary messages often are neither well prepared nor well delivered. Their stories have too much local coloring and, therefore, are not meaningful to the folks at home. Too much time is given to the unimportant details of their work. Seldom do they come to grips with the real issues of the missionary movement of our day. They say little or nothing about the social, economic, and political con-

ditions on the mission field. People come to the meetings hoping
to gain information, but all they get is inspiration. When they're
all through, the audience has learned nothing new. College students are particularly critical at this point. They feel that the
missionaries are not on their wavelength. They speak but don't
communicate. Consequently the younger generation is turned off.

Another criticism is that missionaries are out of touch with
modern life and thought. They are at least ten years behind the
times. When reporting their work they put their best foot forward
and create the impression that all is well, when they, and we,
know better. In their slide and film presentations they show only
the seamy side of life and neglect the more attractive aspects of
the national culture. Missionary prayer letters are no better than
missionary messages. The factual content is often trivial; the lit-
erary style poor. Most prayer letters appeal only to those readers
who have an emotional attachment to the writers.

One of the most persistent criticisms is that the missionary has
been placed on a pedestal. Missionary work has been presented
as the highest of all forms of Christian service; consequently the
missionary is the most spiritual of all Christian workers. At home
he has been revered as a spiritual giant; on the field he has posed
as the Great White Father. But more and more people have visited the mission field and seen the missionary with his hair down.
As a result, they have changed their minds. He may have a heart
of gold; but he has feet of clay. In some instances the clay is
cracked. Thus the missionary has been cut down to size. Indeed
there is real danger that he may be underrated. In some circles
it is assumed that only second-rate students volunteer for missionary service. If one can't make the grade at home, he can
always try the mission field.

The criticism doesn't stop with the missionary; it is carried over
to the mission board. With today's emphasis on personal freedom,
it is not surprising that young people take a dim view of societies
that operate according to definite principles and practices outlined
in the official handbook. The prevailing opinion is that mission
boards are paternalistic, inflexible, even reactionary in their methods of operation. Today's youth have no desire to be placed in a
straitjacket. They want to do their own thing. Certainly they
don't want to sign up for life on the dotted line. This is one rea-

son for the popularity of the short-term program. It affords an opportunity to engage in missionary work without making a long-term commitment.

With all these negative factors working against the missionary, it is little wonder that his image has become marred. But we must get beyond the criticism and try to discover the factors which have contributed to the deteriorating situation. How much of the criticism is valid? How much is objective? How much is subjective? Granted that some of it is subjective, what are some of the factors responsible for the growing criticism?

American society is fast becoming secularized to the point where religion is said to be irrelevant. We are living in a pre-dominantly anthropological age. The universe revolves around a center of gravity called man. Little by little God has been pushed to the perimeter. Today man is the measure of all things. At last he has come of age. He has declared his independence of God. Time was when he used to pray, "Give us this day our daily bread"; but that is unnecessary since he has learned to make cereal out of sawdust. Even our theologians are talking about a "post-Christian era," and calling for "anonymous Christians" to penetrate the "secular city" and there challenge, if not overthrow, the existing "power structures." Salvation is no longer personal but societal. Reconciliation between man and man is more impor-tant than reconciliation between man and God. The church is not a community of saints saved by the grace of God, but a company of sinners trying to work out their own and society's salvation in cooperation with fellow sinners in the world. In fact any dichot-omy between the church and the world is a false one. Both are part of the new humanity, of which Christ is the Head.

Students in Christian colleges are reading and discussing these issues and not a few of them are uncritically accepting the pro-nouncements of the new theology, the new evangelism, and the new morality. To all such students the missionary, with his em-phasis on gospel preaching, soul saving, and church planting, is something of an anachronism. He may have been all right in the nineteenth century; but he is hopelessly out-of-date now. If one is to take the time and pains to live and work abroad, he would do better to sign up with the Peace Corps.

It is common knowledge that Christian colleges are finding it increasingly difficult to get students to accept Christian service assignments. Some colleges have reduced the time students are required to be involved; others have dropped it altogether. The concept of Christian service has been broadened to include every activity from coaching basketball in the local YMCA to supervising day-care centers in the ghetto. Even Christian service as traditionally understood in evangelical circles has been secularized. Little wonder that the Bible-toting missionary feels just a little out of place when he appears on campus.

It should be borne in mind that many of our college students are second- and third-generation evangelicals. They may or may not have the root of the matter in themselves. They have known the facts of the gospel since childhood. They can recite the Scriptures and sing the gospel songs. They are familiar with all the clichés of evangelical Christianity. They can even pray. But they may not be genuine Christians at all. They may be coasting along on the faith and piety of their parents. When they hit college they have all kinds of hang-ups, not the least of which is the challenge of the mission field. Without any foundation to their Christian profession, they can hardly be expected to wax enthusiastic about a Christian vocation. They have just enough evangelicalism to inoculate them against the real thing.

This being so, they are critical not only of the missionary but also of the pastor, His prestige has dropped along with that of the missionary. It is not easy to attract young men into the ministry. It is simply a matter of record that our sharpest young people are not going into the ministry at home, much less into missionary work overseas. The image of the local pastor has been tarnished almost as much as that of the missionary.

There are fewer "rewards" in Christian service than previously was the case. Time was when the minister was the best educated, most honored person in the community. Not so today. Pastors and missionaries have never been well, or even adequately, paid; but at least they enjoyed a measure of prestige. Now they have neither wealth nor prestige.

Then again, Christian work at home and overseas is becoming increasingly difficult. The demands on time and strength are enormous. The burdens are out of all proportion to the privileges. With higher and higher standards of living, more Americans are looking for softer jobs, shorter hours, and higher wages. At one time or another every red-blooded American boy dreams of getting into the major leagues. How can the Christian church compete with Hollywood, Madison Avenue, and the Dallas Cowboys?

It is only fair to say that much present-day criticism of the missionary is ill-informed. It stems from ignorance rather than knowledge. How many critics have read a full-length missionary biography, much less a major work on modern missions? How many have taken the time to talk personally and at length with a well-informed missionary? Few people are sufficiently aware of the enormous progress made in recent years, or of the nature and magnitude of the problems that remain. Missionaries, far from being behind the times, are usually better informed on world affairs than their friends at home.

One other thing ought to be remembered. It is just possible that the negative attitude of some people stems from a guilt complex. They know in their hearts that all is not right between them and the Lord. They may even have a sneaking suspicion that God wants them on the mission field, and they are not prepared to obey. For all such persons, criticism becomes a convenient escape mechanism.

This brings us back to the question at the beginning of the chapter: how can we enhance the missionary image? There are three possible courses of action, depending on the circumstances. The missionary must be educated about some aspects of the situation; the student must be educated about others. There are some circumstances over which we have no control. We will simply have to learn to live with them. Can we get the missionary and the college student together? I think we can; but we must do some groundwork first.

WE MUST EDUCATE THE MISSIONARY

The missionary is not above criticism. Indeed, he should welcome it. One missionary has claimed, "My critics are the unpaid guardians of my soul." This is true. If the criticism is valid, we should welcome it and profit by it. It is a great pity that so few missionaries have an opportunity for frank dialogue with students. The right kind of dialogue might prove beneficial to both sides. Personally, I am persuaded that the younger generation is not so far out as some people think. Their bark is worse than their bite. As for the so-called generation gap, it has been grossly exaggerated by experts who make a living speaking and writing on the subject.

The missionary should realize that he has two strikes against him and act accordingly. Times have changed; he is no longer a hero. If he is to get a hearing, he must earn it.

The missionary should do his best to understand young people and their hang-ups and not be too perturbed when they sound off. It has always been the prerogative of the young to be brash. Today they are hypercritical of society in general and the church in particular. They are not exactly bashful when it comes to expressing their feelings. They no longer respect their elders simply because of their age.

The missionary should know his own limitations and live with them. Not all missionaries are good speakers; and even a missionary who goes over well in a midweek prayer meeting may fall flat on his face in a college chapel. Deputation secretaries would do well to show greater awareness of this problem when lining up speaking engagements for missionaries on furlough. It is true that God can overrule the blunders of His servants, and on at least one occasion He conveyed His message through the bray of an ass; but this should be the exception, not the rule. Other things being equal, it is better not to have any missionary speaker in chapel, than to have a poor one.

Even a good speaker should take nothing for granted. Nobody owes him a hearing. Moreover he has plenty of competition from experts in the entertainment and communication fields. In order to communicate, three factors must be present. First, his topic must be relevant; and relevance is determined by the hearer, not the speaker. Second, every message should be well prepared; and the shorter the message, the longer the preparation. He should not depend on his background or experience, certainly not on the inspiration of the moment. Someone recently remarked that the church is the one remaining institution where a person has the right to speak even when he has nothing to say. Every missionary should see to it that he has something to say. Third, he should articulate as cogently as possible and sit down when he is finished. When a speaker exceeds his allotted time, he immediately loses his audience. A college speaker at the opening of a Spiritual Life Week prefaced his first message with these words: "As I understand it, you and I have a twofold assignment this week. My assignment is to speak; yours is to listen. If you finish your assignment before I finish mine, please raise your hand." It might be a good thing if all audiences had an opportunity to raise their hands!

In many instances the slide presentation is the most painful of all missionary messages. In these days when audiovisual techniques are so sophisticated, there is no excuse for mediocrity in this area. If the missionary doesn't know how to prepare and present an illustrated lecture, he should learn how before starting out on deputation work. The slides are not an end in themselves, but a means to an end. The illustrated lecture is precisely that— an illustrated *lecture*. As in any good lecture, there should be an introduction and a conclusion; and the material between the two should be characterized by continuity. The narrative should run smoothly, logically, and progressively, while the pictures are flashed on the screen for *illustrative purposes only*. It should not be necessary for the speaker to draw attention to the slides; and to explain the slides is to insult the intelligence of the audience. And for goodness' sake, don't end with a sunset scene!

The missionary on furlough must be willing to level with young people, listen to their story, answer their questions, and seek to establish some kind of rapport. If he is unable to answer some of the questions, this should not disturb him. Nobody has all the answers. Young people respect a person who has the courage to say, "I don't know."

We Must Educate the Home Constituency

Not all the blame lies with the missionary. Some of it rests with the folks at home. Somehow we must try to educate them and bring them up to date with regard to modern missions in order to correct, if possible, some misconceptions.

Criticism, if it is to be constructive, must be relevant and meaningful. Whipping a dead horse is an exercise in futility. The outworn criticisms of bygone days should be replaced with insights that reflect up-to-date, mature thinking. We still have people who lambaste missionaries for their shabby appearance, their secondhand cars, their lack of makeup, etc. It we must criticize, let us seize upon substantive issues with some importance and significance. It is by no means certain that if Jesus Christ were to come back today He would feel at home in our affluent society. Certainly He would not wear Florsheim shoes or drive a Mercedes Benz. When He was here before, He declared that a man's life does not consist in the abundance of things that he possesses. He also reminded us that the life is more than meat, and the body than raiment. We all pay lip service to these high concepts, but few of us take them seriously. Why should missionaries be criticized for practicing what the rest of us are content to preach?

The youth in our schools and churches should be encouraged to treat missionaries as they themselves wish to be treated. They demand that they be accepted "as persons" just as they are, with their beads, their beards, and their bell bottoms. This being so, they should be willing to accept the missionary "as a person," in spite of all his idiosyncrasies. If the female missionary is expected to accept the college co-ed with her miniskirt, should not the co-ed accept the missionary with her midi? If the stateside girls have the right to wear what they like, should not the missionary on furlough have the same right? Why should we deny to the missionary the rights that we demand for ourselves? If acceptance is to be genuine, it must be mutual. It cannot be a one-way affair.

Today's youth should recognize that they have an obligation to try to understand and appreciate viewpoints other than their own. It is just possible that they may be wrong and the other fellow right. Missionaries should try to find the wavelength of the younger generation. On the other hand, college students should make an honest effort to locate the wavelength of the missionary. Students are not the only ones with a peculiar wavelength!

College students often complain that missionary speakers "turn them off." Doubtless this is true; but they should remember that they have no monopoly on being turned off. Older people are just as easily turned off by young people! If we are to have genuine dialogue, *both* parties must be turned on, not just the students. One test of our maturity is our ability to listen attentively to the other fellow's point of view. We should not take offense simply because he tosses in a few clichés. Besides, our new clichés may be as offensive to him as his old ones are to us. It is imperative that the lines of communication be kept open in both directions.

College students should beware of discounting the whole missionary enterprise because one or two missionaries may be poor platform personalities. Not all missionaries are dynamic speakers; but the same may be said of pastors. Indeed, not all college professors are dynamic teachers. It should be remembered that it is not always the best speaker or the most glamorous personality who makes the best missionary. There is much more to missionary work than preaching.

Another facet often overlooked is the fact that culture shock is a two-way street. The "reentry" on furlough is often as turbulent as the outward journey some years before. Certainly it takes time, patience, wisdom, and tact to adjust to the American way of life after five years in the Baleim Valley of West Irian. This is especially true in recent years, when life-styles in the Western world are changing so rapidly and so radically. The missionary used to travel by boat. This gave him three or four weeks for orientation. Now he travels by air and arrives at Kennedy International Airport in less than twenty-four hours. The shock of reentry can be traumatic. Today's missionary on furlough deserves our sympathy, not our scorn.

In spite of the fact that the United States is the most powerful country in the world, the American people are rather provincial in their outlook. They are much more interested in their own problems than in the affairs of the United Nations. Judged by their coverage of international news, there are probably not more than a dozen really good newspapers in the whole country. This kind of ethnocentrism is reflected in our attitude toward the missionary and his work. The missionary's world is so far removed from ours that it is difficult for us to show genuine interest in his story. I remember one Foreign Missions Fellowship student leader at a get-acquainted session prior to the annual missionary conference, saying to the missionaries: "Now don't talk too much about your work overseas. Try to say something that will be relevant to the student body."

We in the home constituency must cultivate the ability to appreciate an address on India, Brazil, or Nigeria without demanding that the content be made relevant to us. Naturally the missionary is going to speak about his work, his country, and his people. He assumes that this is what the people want to hear, else why invite him in the first place? It is hardly fair to invite a missionary to speak in church or chapel and then inform him that the audience is really more interested in the claims of the inner city than the needs of the mission field. This is not to say that the latter is more important than the former. Both are equally important. But it is unrealistic to expect any speaker to talk about another person's work.

Some Things Cannot Be Changed

He was a wise man who prayed: "God, grant me the serenity to accept the things I cannot change, the courage to change the things I can, and the wisdom to know the difference." Having educated the missionary and the home constituency, we must realize that there are still some things that we cannot change. They are facts of life, and we must learn to live with them. There is no point in wringing our hands or beating our breasts.

One very potent factor is the influence of the social sciences, especially anthropology. Most anthropologists are humanists; consequently they have only one dimension to their thinking—the horizontal. God is not in all their thoughts. To them religion is a purely social phenomenon, an integral part of culture. Each social group has its own distinctive culture, which presumably is the one best suited to it; else it would not have survived over such a long period of time. No outsider, they argue, has the right to interfere in a people's culture. Cultural mores are neither right nor wrong, moral nor immoral. Any custom that the people regard as good is good for them. All peoples, therefore, should be left to develop their own culture as they see fit without any outside interference.

According to this theory the Christian missionary commits a grave error when he introduces an alien religion. As for converting a person from one faith to another, this is anathema with the anthropologists. Not only is it foolish, because one religion is as good as another; but worse still, it takes the convert out of his social habitat and alienates him from his friends and neighbors. This often leads to ostracism, persecution, and sometimes death. This point of view is presented with great persuasion. The unsuspecting college student, even from an evangelical background, begins to have second thoughts about his erstwhile hero, the missionary. The halo has slipped a notch.

A second factor, equally damaging, is the prevailing notion that in a pluralistic world it is no longer possible to maintain the finality of Jesus Christ or the uniqueness of the Christian faith. Christianity may have served the West well; but Hinduism and Buddhism have served the East equally well. There is little reason to choose between the major religions of mankind. While none is wholly true, all contain elements of truth. Mahatma Gandhi was fond of comparing truth to a tree and the various world religions to its branches. As it takes many branches to make a tree, so it requires many religions to express the truth concerning God, man, life, death, and salvation. For the Christian missionary to claim that he has all the truth and nothing but the truth is an act of arrogance, a form of cultural imperialism.

With this point of view, it is little wonder that present-day historians and anthropologists regard the missionary as an anachronism. He might have served a purpose in the nineteenth century; but he is hopelessly out-of-date in the last half of the twentieth century. So far as the world is concerned, the missionary is hardly a hero.

Another fact is that the missionary has always been regarded as an oddball, not only by the world but to some extent by the church as well. When Justinian von Weltz in the seventeenth century urged the Lutheran churches of Europe to engage in missionary work among the heathen, he met with opposition and contempt. Almost to a man his learned colleagues rose up in indignation, calling him a dreamer, a fanatic, and a heretic. Some fifty years later the faculty of theology at Wittenberg called the Danish-Halle pioneers false prophets because their "orderly vocation was not ascertained." When William Carey first decided on a missionary career, his father declared him mad, and his wife refused to accompany him. She later repented and went, but she proved to be a burden rather than a blessing. If this is what the church thinks of the missionary vocation, what can we expect of the world?

Any man who deliberately turns his back on the amenities of Western civilization and devotes a lifetime of sacrifice and service to a strange and often hostile people who want neither him nor his message, and does it all for a fraction of what he could make for the same work at home, must be regarded as a bit weird. And when he stays on year after year, learning their language, eating their food, adopting their life-style, and finally coming to genuinely appreciate their exotic culture, the mystery only deepens. When he returns to his native land, he inevitably becomes a misfit. The measure of his identification there is the measure of his alienation here.

Thus it comes about that the missionary has been the object of many jokes and the subject of many cartoons. To this day the cartoonists depict the missionary wearing knee socks, Bermuda shorts, and a pith helmet. The fact that he didn't invent these things, wasn't the only one to use them, and has long since discarded them, makes little difference. Fifty years from now the cartoonists will still be drawing the same pictures. It is doubtful if the missionary will ever live down the reputation foisted on him. Once an image—or worse still a caricature—is fixed it is almost impossible to change it.

In this respect the missionary shares the fate of some others in our society—the school marm, the old maid, the mother-in-law, the female driver. All are regarded as "odd" and come in for more than their share of good-humored ridicule. The fact that women are safer drivers than men, and that many spinsters have better integrated personalities than their married sisters, is beside the point. The image is fixed, and they will have to live with it.

The same is true of the missionary. Through the years he too has acquired an image. Today that image is stereotyped beyond repair. He can't change it no matter how hard he tries. He might as well forget the whole business and get on with the job. Without giving way to self-pity, he can take comfort from the fact that his Master, the only perfect Man who ever lived, was misunderstood by His friends and maligned by His enemies. The greatest missionary of all time, the apostle Paul, had to confess that he and his fellow apostles were regarded as the scum of the earth. In spite of his poor image, the modern missionary enjoys a better reputation than either Jesus or Paul.

Another thing to be borne in mind is the fact that we live in a rapidly changing age. There are few heroes in our sophisticated world of the twentieth century; and those we have don't last very long. They are here today and gone tomorrow. The most spectacular heroes of the present century are the astronauts. They have been with us only ten years and already their glamor is beginning to fade. When Neil Armstrong and Edwin Aldrin stepped onto the surface of the moon on July 20, 1969, it was estimated that 500 million persons witnessed the epochal event on worldwide television. When the second pair of astronauts repeated the performance barely four months later, the number of viewers was cut in half. And when the third pair landed on the moon, some television watchers complained to the networks that the broadcast interfered with their favorite soap operas!

The nineteenth century missionaries were heroes, at least to a small circle of friends and supporters. They crossed the seven seas and traveled to the ends of the earth. They visited strange peoples and learned exotic languages. They translated the Scriptures. They built schools and hospitals. They converted savages into saints; and out of this kind of raw material they fashioned the Christian church. They were trailblazers in every sense of the word. To change the metaphor, they were the astronauts of their time. As such they were heroes. But they have had their day in the sun. They are heroes no longer. They leave unnoticed and return unheralded. Moreover, millions of other people are coming and going, and the missionaries are lost in the shuffle. The wonder is not that they lost their glamor but that they managed to retain it as long as they did.

This is no great loss. The glamor was artificial to begin with. It was not part of the original plan. Jesus told His disciples quite plainly what they could expect at the hands of a hostile world. The list included alienation, humiliation, tribulation, persecution, and a host of other equally disagreeable experiences. Nothing was said of glamor or glory, fame or fortune, patronage or praise. Indeed, He warned them to beware of popularity, saying, "Woe unto you, when all men speak well of you!" (Lk 6:26).

The changing attitude toward the missionary is by no means an unmitigated tragedy. With the halo gone, today's missionary can be what his Lord always intended him to be—a servant. In the heyday of colonialism he was a person of stature, a force to be reckoned with. At home he was a hero; on the field he was a leader. Now he is neither hero nor leader—just a plain servant.

This is a good thing, for it forces the missionary to come to grips with the words of the Master: "As my Father hath sent me, even so send I you" (Jn 20:21). And we all know that "the Son of Man came not to be ministered unto, but to minister, and to give his life a ransom for many" (Mt 20:28). Again He said, "If I then, your Lord and Master, have washed your feet; ye also ought to wash one another's feet" (Jn 13:14).

Seldom in history have the followers of Christ taken kindly to the servant role. Like the early disciples, they have jostled for position and hankered after power. Now they are being forced to take a second look at the teachings of Christ and to bring their life and service into line with His.

3

WHERE ARE THE CANDIDATES?

THERE IS HARDLY a mission today that isn't hurting for lack of suitable candidates. Most missions are doing well if they can get enough recruits to maintain their existing institutions, and this they achieve only by accepting an increasing number of short-term missionaries. The old-line denominational boards are rapidly retrenching. Even the faith missions are having a hard time getting as many recruits as they need. One mission which four years ago had 1,350 members now has only 1,230. In 1970 this mission made an urgent appeal for doctors, dentists, and supporting personnel, and stated that certain medical institutions would have to close if these persons could not be found. Other missions, with few exceptions, can tell the same story.

Strangely enough, this situation exists at a time when church membership is at an all-time high and when our Bible schools and Christian colleges are bursting at the seams. We are graduating more Christian students; but we are getting fewer missionary candidates. The highly successful Urbana missionary convention of 1970, with a record twelve thousand students in attendance, may have marked a turning point; but it is still too early to make an evaluation. Urbana generated a tremendous amount of interest and enthusiasm. Will this interest be translated into action, or was Urbana just an evangelical Woodstock? Time will tell.

What is the reason for the decline in missionary recruits from among our evangelical youth? The problem has many ramifications and there is no one, overall answer. The situation is highly complex. An analysis of the problem reveals several contributing factors.

THE POLITICAL FACTOR

One does not have to be a student of political science to know that the world is seething with unrest. Riot and revolution are the order of the day. In some parts of the world governments rise and fall almost with the barometer. During the first decade of independence some twenty-five African countries experienced coups of one kind or another. Some countries have had three or four coups, and the end is not yet.

The situation in Asia has been even worse. Civil wars or wars of liberation have occurred in Malaysia, Philippines, Pakistan, Indonesia, Burma, Laos, Vietnam, and Cambodia. India and Pakistan have gone to war several times over Kashmir and Bangladesh. On mainland China millions of persons have been liquidated as "enemies of the people." Abroad China committed genocide against Tibet and grabbed large chunks of territory from India, Pakistan, and Burma. North and South Korea were locked in bloody conflict in the early 1950s, and a peace treaty has not yet been signed. And what shall we say about Vietnam— the dirtiest conflict of all time?

In the Middle East three times the Arabs have gone to war with Israel. Hardly a week passes without killings on both sides. In Latin America the pattern is much the same—riots, revolutions, palace coups, wars, civil wars, guerrilla activity, and other forms of violence. Since World War II there have been over fifty wars, large and small, in various parts of the world.

This kind of unrest is bound to have an adverse effect on all expatriots living in these countries. Missionaries, because of their location up-country, are especially exposed. The cold war has made American missionaries particularly vulnerable. In Algeria missionaries were accused of being agents of the CIA and expelled. In Zaire (formerly Congo) over two hundred missionaries, mostly Roman Catholic, lost their lives, some of them hacked to pieces and thrown to the crocodiles. In Vietnam six missionaries were killed in the *Tet* offensive; others were held prisoner by the Viet Cong; and still others were accidentally killed by exploding mines. In North Thailand two missionaries were killed by bandits. In Cuba two American missionaries and an unknown number of Cuban pastors spent several years in prison. In Colombia several missionaries and scores of national pastors were killed during *La*

Violencia. In Eastern Nigeria, missionaries were accused of collaborating with the Biafran authorities and expelled from the country. In Indonesia, missionaries and church leaders were marked for death by the Communists. Had the coup of October 1, 1965, been successful, they would have been liquidated. The full story of the 1971 civil war in Bangladesh has not yet been told; but we do know that thousands of persons were killed and some ten million refugees fled to India. Several missionaries were killed; others barely escaped with their lives. A missionary was stabbed to death in Somalia, another in Cameroon. And so it goes from country to country around the world.

During the nineteenth century, in the heyday of colonialism in Africa, the missionaries enjoyed the protection of the European powers. Although the popular cartoons depict missionaries being boiled alive by Africans, comparatively few missionaries met a violent death. They died like flies of malaria, yellow fever, and other diseases; but they were not killed. The colonial governments saw to that. For better or worse, colonialism in Africa ended the slave trade, stopped tribal warfare, and imposed a continentwide peace.

But times have changed. The colonial era is over and the gunboats have been recalled. The missionaries are guests, not hosts. As such they are expected to take joyfully the spoiling of their goods and, if need be, to hazard their lives for the sake of the gospel. The changed political climate is forcing the Christian missionaries to be more Christian, to do what the first-century missionaries did—trust in the Lord and look to local magistrates for protection.

And this comes about at a time when we in the Western world are told to take it easy, to play it safe. No longer are we exhorted to build our cities at the foot of Vesuvius, but to protect ourselves and our families from every form of danger. Health plans, medical checkups, insurance policies, unemployment compensation, social security, and pension plans are built-in safeguards designed to protect us from the hard knocks of a competitive society.

Physical well-being, financial security, material prosperity, peace and contentment, law and order—these are the main ingredients that make up the affluent society that is America. The individual is to be pampered and protected from the cradle to the grave. Dentistry, surgery, and now childbirth, are all rendered painless. Even Band-Aids must be "ouchless."

Can we blame our youth, reared in this kind of climate, if they hesitate for a lifetime of service overseas, especially if they are married and have children to consider? To a greater degree than they or we realize, the American way of life has conditioned them to ease and comfort rather than to hardship and danger. It seems safe to assume that this is one of the factors that give pause to modern youth as they consider living and working abroad.

THE EDUCATIONAL FACTOR

It is common knowledge that the United States leads the world in higher education. In other countries a college career is a luxury reserved for the favored few. Here in the United States of America more than 50 per cent of all high school graduates go on to college, and the figure is rising every year. With more and better educated young people, we ought to have more, rather than fewer, college grads volunteering for missionary service. But what are the facts?

One outstanding Christian college sent ninety-nine members of the 1951 graduating class to the mission field. A decade later the number dropped to twenty-nine. Five years later, in 1966, only sixteen graduates entered missionary service. And this college is not unusual. Other Christian colleges have witnessed the same trend.

What is the reason for this? Three things are to be noted. First, there is the age-old battle between zeal and knowledge. Many a freshman enters college with a heart on fire for the Lord and eagerly anticipates the day when he can enter full-time Christian service. All goes well for a time, but after a while he discovers that his interest in spiritual things is beginning to wane. He finds general psychology more exciting than Christian ethics. Plato's *Republic* seems to be more interesting than Leviticus or Jeremiah. The chapel speakers are not a match for college professors. The Foreign Missions Fellowship meetings can't compete with the give-and-take of the classroom situation. Moreover, he is encouraged to rethink his theological position so that his faith may be his own and not that of his parents. He is challenged to give up his narrow view of the Christian life with its rigid categories of black and white, right and wrong, and to embrace a more sophisticated understanding of the wholeness of life. Gone are the former dichotomies between the secular and the sacred, between work and prayer, between service and witness. As for a missionary call—forget it. All Christians are missionaries.

During his first year he makes a gallant effort to maintain his personal devotions, his Christian service, and his missionary interest; but the odds are against him. The pressure of the academic rat race, the indifference and cynicism of the upperclassmen, the avant-garde thinking of some faculty members, the secular atmosphere of the classroom, the profane nature of the bull sessions combine to dull his missionary vision and sap his spiritual strength. Little by little he takes on the complexion of his environment. By graduation time he is a different person. He has exchanged zeal for knowledge. His faith may remain intact; but he has lost the desire to share it with others.

In theory there is no good reason why we must settle for this artificial dichotomy between zeal and knowledge. Why cannot we have zeal and knowledge all wrapped up in one package? Why must one man be an evangelist and another man a scholar? Now and again we find both qualities in one person. Samuel Zwemer had the mind of a scholar and the heart of an evangelist. He was a missionary par excellence. Alas, we haven't had many Samuel Zwemers.

Second, there is the problem of "wasting" one's talents on the mission field. Every mission board is crying out for better-educated missionaries. Why don't they get them? One reason is that the more education a man has under his belt, the less likely he is to give serious consideration to the claims of a missionary career. This is not to suggest that he is too proud to enter missionary service. He just assumes that there is not enough scope on the mission field for the many talents he has acquired.

For instance, if he has a doctor's degree in theology he will naturally want to teach in an institution where his advanced education can be used to the greatest advantage. If he has any ambition at all—and who wants him if he doesn't—he will want to engage in research and writing as well as teaching; but for that he will need to be in a prestigious institution or have access to the resources of a large university.

But how can he do this if he teaches on the mission field, where the average theological seminary has twenty-six students, more than half of whom have only a high school education? The physical facilities will leave much to be desired, and the library—the heart of any school—will probably not have more than five thousand volumes, most of them out of date.

The same thing applies to a medical doctor. If he stays at home, he will be able to function in a beautiful hospital with the latest equipment and all kinds of modern facilities. If he opts for the mission field, he may end up in a small hospital with inferior equipment and a third-rate staff. In all probability he will be the only doctor on the staff. In addition to his professional duties as a doctor he will have to be a jack-of-all trades, ready and willing to do many menial tasks beneath the dignity of the average doctor in the United States.

The more education a person acquires, the more options he has. The more options he has, the less likely he is to end up on the mission field. He has too many attractive stateside offers. His friends and relatives, and sometimes the church, will offer him inducements to remain at home.

There is one other snag. Higher education is increasingly costly, and many students at the close of their college career find themselves up to their eyes in debt. No reputable mission board will accept a candidate with that kind of millstone around his neck. The debt must be wiped out before he can leave for the field. To do this, the candidate must find a job. If he goes into law, or medicine, or business, he will be able to repay his debts in a comparatively short time; but if he takes up any form of full-time Christian service, he is likely to require anywhere from two to five years to liquidate them. In the meantime, he has married, started a family, and gotten his roots down pretty far in American soil. By the time he is free of debt, he may decide that the Lord wants him here at home.

Higher education is a splendid thing. It is producing *better* missionaries; but it isn't producing *more* missionaries.

THE ECONOMIC FACTOR

No one in his right mind would equate the American way of life with the kingdom of God; but it is simply a matter of record that we do have the highest standard of living in the world, despite pockets of poverty in the ghettos of our larger cities. The youth of today, born after World War II, know nothing of the depression of the 1930s or the wartime austerity of the early 1940s. They have been born and bred in the lap of luxury. Through no fault of their own, they are the product of the most affluent age in human history.

Several years ago *Time* magazine reported that 35 percent of the high school boys and 25 percent of the girls have part-time jobs. They have three times as much money as their counterparts prior to World War II. Teenagers have twenty-four billion dollars a year to spend, and with it they have created a whole new subculture of their own. Madison Avenue is gearing much of its advertising to this rapidly expanding market with almost limitless possibilities. When the author started to work in 1926, he made $30 a month. Today his sixteen-year-old son is making $100 a week! Of course, the cost of living has gone up in the intervening years, but hardly 1300 percent!

Let's face it. Young people going to the mission field today have more to "give up" than we did a generation ago. When I left for China in 1935, I had very little to part with. I had no stereo, no radio, no television, no Polaroid camera, no tape recorder, and certainly no car. All I had was a secondhand portable typewriter, and that I took with me.

We hear a great deal today about the large metropolitan centers on the mission field with their international airports, their high-rise apartments, their air-conditioned office buildings, their public libraries, their mammoth stadiums, their wide boulevards, their modern universities, and their morning and evening traffic jams. This is all true. The fact remains, however, as Barbara Ward Jackson has warned us in *Policy for the West,* that the economic gap between the "have" nations and the "have-not" nations is widening with every passing year. In spite of four fairly successful Five Year Plans, the standard of living in India is not much higher than it was twenty years ago. The increase in population has just about wiped out the increase in productivity.

We usually think of the missionary pioneers as making a great sacrifice when they went to Africa and Asia in the nineteenth century. This is not altogether true. When Hudson Taylor arrived in China he didn't find any indoor plumbing, central heating, electric light, or telephone service. So what? He didn't have them back in England either. Where then was the sacrifice? I dare say that the economic gap between England and China in 1853 was not as great as the gap between China and the United States today. There is a sense in which today's missionary candidates make greater material sacrifices than their predecessors a hundred years ago. This should be borne in mind when we are tempted to criticize the younger generation for their reluctance to forego the amenities of Western technological civilization.

Nor have the churches in this country helped us very much at this point. They too have been caught up in the mad rush to increase their budgets, landscape their properties, and beautify their buildings with new and expensive carpets on the floors, cushions on the pews, and curtains on the windows. On Sunday mornings we are exhorted to be thankful for all the good things of life which God has given us richly to enjoy; but seldom does the preacher remind us of the words of our Lord: "A man's life consisteth not in the abundance of things which he possesseth" (Lk 12:15). Little wonder that Christian young people think twice before volunteering to join the ranks of the "poverty-stricken" missionaries whose pictures adorn the bulletin board in the foyer.

THE VOCATIONAL FACTOR

Today's youth are vocation conscious to a degree not known in previous generations. It begins in grade school and continues through high school. Various kinds of aptitude tests are given and evaluated by qualified counselors. The student is called in, and the counselor proceeds to interpret the results of the test. Most of these counselors are competent and conscientious. The problem is that they have only one dimension to their thinking— the horizontal. God is not in all their thoughts. No attempt is made to relate the student and his talents to the will of God or the work of the church. In fact, there seems to be a conspiracy to keep the church and its vocations out of the picture. At one time, the Department of Education of the Commonwealth of Pennsylvania published a list of occupations which the school counselors are prepared to discuss with the student. The list contained 154 different occupations, all the way from agriculture to zoology; but occupations relating to church, mission, and religion were all conspicuous by their absence. Some guidance counselors have been known to go out of their way to try to dissuade high school seniors from applying to Bible school.

Young people used to take their cue from their parents and their pastor; but no longer so. They are more likely to follow the advice of the guidance counselors at school. After all, the tests are scientific, and the counselors are trained professionals. One very successful pastor in the Philadelphia area told the author that he has had a hundred young people go away to college. For most of them he was asked to fill out a questionnaire or write a letter of reference; but only six of them ever bothered to seek his advice about their college career or their lifework.

We are living in an anthropocentric age. Man is the measure of all things. He has come of age. He is quite capable of solving his own problems and making his own choices. He doesn't need God to tell him what to do with his life. He can discover that much better and more quickly by an aptitude test. All unconsciously the Christian student is infected with this spirit of independence. He wants to do his own thing. He doesn't want anybody to tell him what to do.

Some years ago I was talking with a college senior who was within three months of graduation and still had no idea what he was going to do. He was a Christian boy who at one time had entertained serious thoughts of entering the ministry. Now he was not sure. So I asked him: "Jim, do you ever pray about this matter? Have you ever asked God to guide you with regard to your lifework?"

He replied, "Oh, I take God for granted; He is always in the back of my mind. I make my decisions as best I can in the light of what I know about myself, and I trust Him to stop me if I go wrong."

There is nothing wrong with aptitude tests or guidance counselors per se. What the counselors and students don't seem to know is that God is not necessarily restricted in His choice of missionary candidates to those whose aptitude tests show a penchant for preaching or whose personality profiles reveal a meek and quiet spirit. If the twelve apostles had been subjected to a modern aptitude test, I wonder how many of them would have made the grade. Peter would have been ruled out; he was too fickle. Thomas would have been turned down; he was too skeptical. Paul would have been sent home; he was too intolerant.

No man can be a disciple unless he is prepared to acknowledge the lordship of Jesus Christ without any ifs, ands, or buts. He demands unconditional surrender followed by total obedience. When that matter is taken care of, then He decides what to do with our gifts and talents.

It is precisely at this point that many young Christians have a real hang-up. They have a sneaking suspicion that if they make a total surrender to Jesus Christ they will never be genuinely happy again. He will force them into His mold, and they will end up by being square pegs in round holes—and who wants that? They assume that He will make them do the very thing they have always vowed they would never do. In other words, He will rub their noses in the dirt just to prove His lordship.

Nothing could be further from the truth. When a person surrenders to Jesus Christ, he does not lose his life, he gains it (Mt 10:39). On the contrary, the person who seeks to hold on to his life, ends up by losing it. Self-fulfillment comes by way of self-denial. Jesus said, "Take my yoke upon you, and learn of me; for I am meek and lowly in heart: and ye shall find rest unto your souls. For my yoke is easy, and my burden is light" (Mt 11:29-30).

Time and again Paul stated that he was an apostle by the will of God, not by his own choice. God in His sovereignty reserves the right to deploy His servants as He sees fit. He has a master plan for every life which He has redeemed with the blood of Christ. The psalmist said, "As for God, his way is perfect . . . [He] maketh my way perfect" (Ps 18:30, 32). He makes no mistakes. He is in possession of all the facts. He doesn't need to consult the charts or graphs. He understands the individual better than the individual understands himself. His will is always "good, and acceptable, and perfect" (Ro 12:2). He knows not only where the servant is needed most, but also where he will function best. If God decides to make a missionary out of a musician, or a preacher out of a plumber, or an evangelist out of an engineer, who are we to say Him nay? "Shall the thing formed say to him that formed it, Why hast thou made me thus?" (Ro 9:20).

THE THEOLOGICAL FACTOR

The entire missionary movement is based on three presuppositions rooted in the Christian revelation. First, that man is lost and needs to be saved. Second, that salvation is found only in Jesus Christ. Third, that in order to be saved it is necessary to understand and believe the gospel. Almost to a man the missionaries of the nineteenth century accepted these propositions without any mental reservations. To them the Christian mission was a serious business. The "heathen," as they called them, were lost and on their way to hell; and it was imperative that someone take the gospel to them without delay. They fully understood the implications of Paul's words, "Knowing therefore the terror of the Lord, we persuade men" (2 Co 5:11). Hudson Taylor said, "If I had a thousand lives, I should give them all to China." Henry Martyn on his arrival in India said, "Now let me burn out for God." Melville Cox, the first Methodist missionary to Liberia, died within four months of his arrival. His last words were, "Let a thousand fall before Africa be given up."

This rare phenomenon was known as a "passion for souls." It has been the hallmark of all the great missionaries through the ages—Francis Xavier, Raymond Lull, David Brainerd, Mary Slessor, Sadhu Sundar Singh, John Sung, Dan Crawford, and a host of others. Greatest of them all was the apostle Paul, who said, "I could wish that myself were accursed from Christ for my brethren, my kinsmen according to the flesh" (Ro 9:3).

This sense of urgency is missing from modern missionary literature. Few references are made to the lostness of the heathen. Indeed, in liberal circles the notion that men without Christ are lost has long since been abandoned. The emphasis is on love to the exclusion of everything else. God is too good to consign any man to hell. Christ died for all; therefore all are saved whether or not they know it. The missionary's job is not to call for repentance and faith, but simply to announce the good news that all men are now part of the new humanity of which Christ is the Head.

Even in evangelical circles the note of urgency is missing.

There are those in the evangelical camp who are having second thoughts about many things, one of them being the fate of the heathen. They are not prepared to say that all the heathen will be saved; neither are they persuaded that all will be lost. They take a somewhat ambivalent stand halfway between the two extremes. They like to think that somehow God will devise ways and means of getting the non-Christian masses into heaven through the back door. They contend that the idea of eternal punishment is repugnant to the modern mind: consequently if Christianity is to be made palatable to twentieth century man, eternal punishment must go.

This point of view is particularly prevalent among Christian students. A sampling of the views represented at the Urbana missionary conference in 1967 revealed the fact that only 38 percent of all the delegates believed that anyone who does not hear the gospel is eternally lost.

There is no doubt whatever that failure to take seriously the wrath of God is a major factor in the falling off of missionary candidates in our day. Obviously, if the heathen are not eternally lost there is no compelling reason why we should break our necks to share the gospel with them; they don't really need it. We might just as well sit back and agree with the anthropologists who say, "Leave them alone; they are happy as they are." If the heathen are not lost without Christ, the Christian mission is reduced to the status of the Peace Corps.

THE SPIRITUAL FACTOR

Perhaps the greatest weakness of the evangelical churches of our day is their failure to declare the whole counsel of God. They are preaching the gospel, but it is an emasculated gospel. A. W. Tozer called it "instant Christianity." He said:

> It is hardly a matter of wonder that the country that gave the world instant tea and instant coffee should be the one to give it instant Christianity. . . . It cannot be denied that it was American fundamentalism that brought instant Christianity to the gospel churches. . . . By instant Christianity I mean the kind found almost everywhere in gospel circles and which is born of the notion that we may discharge our total obligation to our own souls by one act of faith, or at most by two, and be relieved thereafter of

all anxiety about our own spiritual condition. . . . By trying to pack all of salvation into one experience, or two, the advocates of instant Christianity flaunt the law of development which runs through all nature. They ignore the sanctifying effects of suffering, cross-carrying and practical obedience. They pass by the need for spiritual training, the necessity of forming right religious habits and the need to wrestle against the world, the flesh and the devil.[1]

We play up the love, joy, and peace aspects of the gospel. We preach justification by faith. We rejoice in the forgiveness of sins and the assurance of salvation, all of which is blessedly and wonderfully true. We have even gone so far as to talk about separation from the world, though we are hearing less and less of this, but we have said little or nothing about the other side of the gospel: persecution, tribulation, sorrow, suffering, and shame. We have talked about living for Christ, but we have said little about dying with Christ, suffering for Christ, or obedience to Christ. We talk about self-fulfillment; Jesus talked about self-denial. Indeed, He went so far as to say that self-denial and cross-bearing are at the very heart of the gospel and that a man cannot be a Christian without them.

In many instances the only challenge given to our young people is the challenge to "give their hearts to Christ." This is understood to be a once-for-all transaction, not a lifetime commitment leading to allegiance to the person of Christ, obedience to the will of Christ, and involvement in the cause of Christ.

Many of the activities planned for our young people are designed to keep them off the streets, to give them something to do, to keep them out of mischief, to provide them with entertainment under Christian auspices. They are not altogether to blame for this sad state of affairs. As parents we have brought them up on a diet of pablum. As teachers we have failed to declare the whole counsel of God. As pastors we have preached an emasculated gospel.

Don't misunderstand me. I am not against entertainment, especially under Christian auspices. Our young people are gregarious like everyone else. They have social needs which must be satisfied if they are to live a well-rounded life and become

1. A. W. Tozer, *That Incredible Christian* (Harrisburg, Penn.: Christian Pubns., 1964), pp. 24-25.

well-integrated personalities. My concern is that so many of our evangelical churches are content to provide a program of social entertainment. Not many of them provide a program of spiritual training. They have their meetings, to be sure. Now and again they give their testimony; but usually it is given in and to their own group. There is no interaction with the unbelieving world. There is no persecution, no hostility, not even opposition. Open-air meetings, house-to-house visitation, tract distribution, rescue missions, hospital visitation, prison work—all are conspicuous today by their absence. Even good, solid Bible study and prayer are hard to find. Most of our high school students have part-time jobs with their own income, which in some instances is rather a tidy sum of money. But not many of them tithe their income. They are not taught to tithe; they are not expected to tithe. If they put into the offering plate enough to cover the expense of their own activities they are doing well. In some instances the church picks up the tab.

If our young people have no outlet for their spiritual energies while they are in high school, what is going to make them suddenly seek such outlets when they get to college? If they have not attended prayer meeting in church, why should they attend the missionary prayer band in college?

It is no secret that our Bible schools and Christian colleges are finding it increasingly difficult to persuade students to accept Christian service assignments. About the only event that takes our young people out of the church and into the community for Christian service is carol singing on Christmas Eve, and that usually ends up in the church with hot chocolate and cake. This is not the way to train missionary candidates.

That young people today must be entertained, must be accommodated, must be patronized, must be given preferential treatment, is by no means an established fact. They will follow a leader if he is the right man. They want a leader who will inspire and challenge them, not by a weary, endless series of peptalks, but by the quiet example of his own life, the integrity of his own heart, the dynamic of his own energy, the contagion of his own courage. They will respond to a cause if it is big enough. They want a cause that is worth living for, and if necessary worth dying for. They want a program of action. Young people all over the world

—Communists, nationalists, socialists, and atheists—are on the march, giving themselves without reserve and without regret to social and political crusades which tax their strength and, in some cases, take their lives. Alas, that the Christian church, and especially the evangelical wing of that church, has not found a way to challenge the Christian young people of our day.

The Success Factor

The American people are success oriented. They play to win, and if they don't win—and win big—they are ready to throw in the towel. They will support a team as long as it is winning; but when the batters go into a slump the fans begin to boo. In 1969 the Chicago Cubs all but had the pennant wrapped up at the end of August. Then came the September slump when the team lost eight or nine games in a row. During the last game with the New York Mets, the "loyal" fans were so infuriated that they littered the field with debris and finally stopped the game by throwing a stink bomb on the infield grass.

This competitive spirit, this compulsion to win, is carried over into all areas of American life—business, medicine, law, education, and politics. The winner runs off with everything, while the loser is left holding a bag with holes in the bottom. Who wants to be a loser?

Nor has organized religion altogether escaped the irresistible force of the never-ending merry-go-round. Denominational organizations have their charts and graphs, and local churches have their annual reports. Church membership and Sunday school attendance, home and hospital visitation, baptisms and confirmations, tithes and offerings—all must show an increase if the congregation is going to continue to support the program. Certainly if the pastor expects an increment in his salary he had better come up with a "successful" annual report.

How does all this affect the potential missionary candidate? Much will depend on his own maturity and his knowledge of the missionary enterprise with all its victories and failures. Much will also depend on his choice of a mission, the field to which he will be assigned, and the niche he will fill when he gets there. Depending on how one arranges his facts, he can paint either a very bright or a very dismal picture. He can elaborate on the ex-

citement of missionary life, or he can underscore the frustrations
of missionary work. Both are facts of life on the mission field.

It is correct to say that the overall picture is not one of perpetual action, excitement, and results. The American concept of
success is becoming more elusive with every passing year. If
success is to be equated with adventure, the young missionary is
doomed to failure; for there are no unexplored areas left in the
world. If success is to be equated with prestige, he is in for a
disappointment, for the day of the Great White Father is past.
If success is to be equated with glamor, he might as well stay at
home; for the glamor has long since gone out of the missionary
enterprise. If success is to be equated with a mansion on the hill
and a houseful of servants, he might as well forget it; for the day
of the mission compound is fast fading. If success is to be equated
with the exercise of ecclesiastical power, he is in for a shock.
Today's missionary is the servant, not the boss, of the national
church. If success is to be equated with numerical results he may
or may not be happy; for some peoples are responsive and others
are resistant.

To make matters worse, the prophets of doom are telling us
that we have entered upon a post-Christian era, that the ratio of
Christians to non-Christians in the world is steadily decreasing,
and that the modern missionary movement of the last two centuries came to an end with the demise of the colonial system of
which it was a part. Missionaries on furlough add to the cacoph-
ony by announcing from the housetops that time is short and
doors are closing. What person, young or old, wants to support a
dying cause? The Christian student can be forgiven if he con-
cludes that the Peace Corps is a better risk than the Christian
mission.

The Image Factor

Image is one of the most important concepts in American life
today. Every institution that deals with the public is deeply concerned about the image it projects. If the image is good, it is
likely to succeed. If it is bad, it is almost sure to fail. Madison
Avenue spends billions of dollars every year in a mammoth effort
to persuade the American consumer that today's products are
better than they really are. The image, it would seem, is more

important than the reality. Such diverse groups as labor and management, government and business, the Pentagon and the police force—all are deeply concerned about their image. Politicians are particularly vulnerable at this point. Even religious organizations are not without their concern. Christian colleges, theological seminaries, and mission boards are engaging in various kinds of self-study programs, often with outside professional help, in an effort to enhance their image in the eyes of their constituencies. There is no doubt about it; we are image conscious to an unusual degree.

It is particularly distressing that at a time when other people are polishing their image the missionary image should appear so tarnished. Traditionally the missionary has been the object of adulation on the part of the sending churches. Even the world, while doubting his wisdom and deploring his superiority complex, has paid tribute to his courage, devotion, and zeal. When the missionaries went out they were given a gala send-off, showered with gifts, and supported by the faithful. When they returned from the remote parts of the earth, they were given a hero's welcome. Many of them were given honorary degrees by the most prestigious universities in the Western world. Others were received in audience by the kings and queens of Europe. Still others were honored by their own and other governments with the highest decorations in the realm.

Now when missionaries return they are fortunate to get their picture in the hometown newspaper. There are just too many of them around. They are no longer the only pebble on the beach. Others also go abroad, achieve fame, and return home to the plaudits of their countrymen. The greatest competition comes from the Peace Corps.

With few exceptions, the missionaries are no longer doing exploits. The pioneer days are over. There are no more lands to explore; few savages remain to be civilized. Consequently when they return home they have no hair-raising stories to tell. If perchance some natural disaster occurs on the mission field, the news media have already provided full coverage on the six o'clock news. The missionaries are no longer the bearers of strange and exciting tales. At long last they have been cut down to size.

Moreover, the fact that the American life-style is changing so rapidly tends to make the missionary feel, if not look, hopelessly out-of-date. In fact the reentry may involve a greater degree of culture shock than the outward journey did four years before. It may take him weeks to get back on the wavelength of American youth. In the meantime, his attempts at communication are not a howling success. And what shall be said about the matter of dress? Even if he had the money for a completely new set of clothes, he would feel like a polar bear on the equator in some outfits. As for the female missionary, she would require the daring of a Raquel Welch to appear in public in a miniskirt.

Nor can the missionary honestly tell the home constituency that he is wowing, much less winning, the world. The work is hard, the hours are long, the problems are great, the results are meager. He is building churches not blazing trails. He is translating the Scriptures, teaching classes, training leaders, none of which is very exciting. Consequently when he gets up to speak in chapel, he doesn't knock the ball out of the park. He does well to get it past the infield. College students looking for a success story are likely to be turned off.

From almost every point of view today's missionary has two strikes against him when he faces the home constituency. Through no fault of his, the image has been tarnished; and there doesn't seem to be any way to refurbish it except to reeducate the supporters here at home.

If the missionary image is tarnished, what shall we say about the image of the mission board? Mission boards, being part of the establishment, come in for their full share of youthful antipathy towards the status quo. They are thought of as being conservative, inflexible, paternalistic, and reactionary. Mission boards are still thinking in the old categories and are not open to new ideas. They cling tenaciously to the outmoded principles and practices of the past and refuse to experiment with new methods and policies. In a word, the mission boards are simply "not with it."

Doubtless the picture is often overdrawn; but the fact remains that this is the image in the minds of many of our evangelical youth. Of course some missions are more progressive than others; but all missions should from time to time take a hard look at their total operation to make sure that they are keeping abreast of the fast-moving times in which we live. Our message is eternal and therefore unchanging. We tamper with that at our peril. But there is nothing sacred about our methods.

It would be wrong to close this chapter without noting recent indications that missionary recruiting may be at a turning point. Several mission boards report a sizable increase in the number of applications received. There is no doubt that the Holy Spirit is working in unusual ways at the present time. Tens of thousands of persons have been won to Christ through the Jesus Movement. Almost a hundred thousand persons, most of them in their teens and early twenties, attended Explo 72 in Dallas. Enrollment in the Bible colleges is up 7.66 percent this year over 1971. The spiritual tone in the Christian liberal arts colleges is reported to be the best in many years. If this kind of spiritual renewal continues, an increasing number of young people will be offering themselves for missionary service. Revival at home always has resulted in increased interest in missions overseas.

4

THE TRUTH ABOUT DROPOUTS

ONE OF THE PROBLEMS confronting the missionary enterprise has been that of dropouts. This should cause no great surprise, since the Christian missionary is engaged in a spiritual warfare that dates back to the Garden of Eden, when our first parents rebelled against God and joined forces with Satan. Ever since that time there have been two kingdoms in the world—the kingdom of God and the kingdom of Satan. These two kingdoms are mutually antagonistic, and the warfare going on between them will continue to the end of time.

Every Christian is part of this warfare, but the missionary, by the very nature of his work, is in the forefront of the battle. Every step takes him deeper and deeper into enemy territory. In one sense, these two kingdoms are worldwide in scope; but each has its own areas of special strength.

True conversion is much more than "deciding for Christ." Whether men realize it or not, the transaction has cosmic significance. When Paul received his commission from God he was told that he was to go to the Gentiles "to open their eyes, and to turn them from darkness to light, and from the power of Satan unto God" (Ac 26:18). The supreme task of the missionary is to bring men to acknowledge the universal lordship of Christ. When they do this they are said to have been delivered from the power of darkness and translated into the kingdom of God (Col 1:13). They cannot belong to both kingdoms at the same time. They can turn to God only if they forsake their idols (1 Th 1:9).

Satan, as the god and prince of this world, is not likely to let his vassals go without a life-and-death struggle. This is certainly true of the devotees of the non-Christian religions, who in a special way are under the power of demonic forces. In many places Satan is not only the object of fear, but of worship as well. Spiritism is rampant in France, Brazil, and other countries. Even in "Christian" America there are now Satan churches where worship is knowingly offered to Satan.

In all parts of the world the Christian missionary comes face to face with demonic systems which for thousands of years have been an integral part of the kingdom of Satan. As a soldier of the cross, he is a threat to this kingdom of evil. As an emissary of light, he is in opposition to all the "rulers of the darkness of this world" (Eph 6:12). The missionary's ultimate quarrel is not with humanism, nationalism, communism, or any other earthly system, but with Satan himself. In the words of Paul, he wrestles "not against flesh and blood, but against principalities, against powers . . . against spiritual wickedness in high places" (Eph 6:12). Like his Master before him, he must first bind the strong man (Satan) before he can spoil his goods (Mt 12:29).

This being so, we should expect to encounter casualties. It is impossible to have war without them. Our only hope is to keep them as light as possible. The casualties are not all physical. Some of them are moral, others are mental, and still others are spiritual. Regardless of their nature, the casualties reflect the fact that we are engaged in a life-and-death struggle between the kingdom of light and the kingdom of darkness.

In the early years of the modern missionary movement the casualty rate was excessively high, especially in Africa, which came to be known as the "White Man's Grave." In Sierra Leone the Church Missionary Society lost 53 missionaries in the first twenty-nine years. In 1900 during the Boxer Rebellion in China, 189 Protestant missionaries and their children were killed. The general situation has gradually improved with the passing of the years, and there have been fewer martyrs. One major setback occurred in Zaire, where 209 missionaries were killed between 1960 and 1965, all but 30 being Roman Catholics.

When we speak of casualties today, however, we refer to missionary dropouts—those who for one reason or another failed to complete the term of service for which they signed up. Much has been said in recent years about these casualties, and the statistics quoted have been rather frightening. Some estimates suggest that 40 percent of the missionaries do not return for their second term of service. Other estimates run as high as 60 percent. Missionaries themselves have been known to quote such figures. What are the facts? Does anyone really know?

To the author's knowledge only two significant studies have been made of missionary dropouts. One of these was done by Dr. Clyde W. Taylor, Executive Secretary of the Evangelical Foreign Missions Association, and the other by the Missionary Research Library of New York. The findings of both studies were remarkably close. Both set the dropout rate at about 15 percent at the end of six years service. In other words, 15 percent of the missionaries failed to return to the field for a second term of service. This is a far cry from the inflated figures that have been bandied about with all the abandonment of confetti at a wedding. Alas, to this day the inflated figures are still being quoted. Apparently people are not taking the time to check the reports, but rather are content to pass on what they hear from others.

Part of the reason for the inflated figures is the fact that in past years the dropout figures included everybody who failed to return to the field *regardless of the reason.* Included in the figures were four categories: retirements, deaths, short-term missionaries completing contracts, and career missionaries with twenty or more years of service. These four categories, termed normally-anticipated withdrawals (the new word for casualties), are no longer regarded as dropouts and therefore should not be included in a study of dropouts. Obviously it is unfair to include in the dropout list those who gave forty or fifty years to missionary service and died in the harness or retired to the homeland. But in the past such figures were included. The word *dropout* today includes only presumably avoidable withdrawals. These are genuine dropouts. What are the figures for these withdrawals?

The study made by the Missionary Research Library was conducted in the mid-1960s and covered the decade from 1953 through 1962.[1] It is the most scientific study ever made of the subject; and its findings are most instructive. The study included 1,409 casualties reported during the decade by thirty-six mission boards. Denominational missions and faith missions, large and

1. Helen L. Bailey and Herbert C. Jackson, *A Study of Missionary Motivation, Training, and Withdrawal (1953-1962)* (New York: Missionary Research Library, 1965). Statistical charts from this study are given at the end of this chapter.

small, were included in the survey. Sixteen of the missions were large, twenty were small. Together they represented 4,970 missionaries. During the ten-year period these thirty-six missions reported 1,409 dropouts, which works out at 28.3 percent for ten years, which is much better than generally believed. Certainly it is a vast improvement on the figure of 40 to 60 percent who are reported not to return to the field after their first furlough.

Apparently one's educational background has little to do with the dropout rate. Bible school graduates account for 28.6 percent of the dropouts, and college graduates 30.9 percent. The study gives no clue as to the ratio of these two categories to the total missionary force of 4,970, however; so we do not know whether the dropouts in these two categories are higher or lower than their numbers would warrant.

It would be interesting to know which category of missionary—evangelistic, educational, or medical—has the highest dropout rate; but this is not possible because almost 30 percent of the respondents failed to indicate the category in which they belonged. The absence of this information throws the study out of kilter at that point.

More accurate is that part of the report that deals with the geographical breakdown of the study. The dropout rate for Africa is abnormally high. Africa represents only 26 percent of the total number of missionaries, but accounts for 33 percent of the dropouts. Doubtless the mass evacuation of Zaire in 1960 helps to explain the high figure for Africa. Asia, on the other hand, with 53 percent of the missionaries, contributed only 44 percent of the dropouts. The more stable political conditions in that continent would explain the good showing there. If the study had covered the China debacle of 1949-51, the figure would have been much higher.

The figures for Europe are interesting. Until recently Europe was not regarded as a mission field, consequently the number of missionaries there is not large—about 1,500 from North America at the present time. But the dropout rate is relatively high. Although Europe has only 1.5 percent of the total number of missionaries included in the study, it accounts for 2.4 percent of the dropouts, which means that the dropout rate there is 60 percent higher than it should be as compared with other areas.

This is somewhat surprising. One would expect the dropouts in Europe to be low because of the many favorable conditions existing there. European culture has much in common with our own. Its languages are much easier to learn than the more complex languages of Africa or Asia. The education of missionaries' children is not the problem it is in other areas. The food and climate are much like what the missionaries were accustomed to here in the homeland. Politics in Europe is less turbulent than in Africa and Asia, with the result that there has never been even a partial evacuation of the missionaries. How then are we to explain the abnormally high dropout rate in Europe? The explanation is simple: Europe has proved to be one of the more resistant mission fields of the world.

The reason is found in the religious climate prevailing in Europe. In the Roman Catholic countries, such as Spain, Portugal, Belgium, and Italy, the Protestants are a tiny, sometimes persecuted, minority. Religious freedom as we understand it simply does not exist, though the situation has improved considerably since Vatican II. In Protestant Europe the vast majority of people belong to the Lutheran or Anglican state churches. Fewer than 5 percent attend church regularly, but they consider themselves good Christians even though they don't work at it. Children are baptized and confirmed in the church; young people are married in the church; and old people are buried from the church. That is the extent of their Christianity. They have just enough to inoculate them against the real thing. Consequently they have no sense of spiritual need, and when the evangelical missionary from North America comes along with his emphasis on individual conversion through personal faith in Jesus Christ, he is apt to be regarded with suspicion if not treated with contempt. The unchurched people of Europe—and they number one hundred million—pride themselves on the high degree of their culture as compared with America's "Coca Cola" culture. They are quite happy with their humanism, skepticism, and materialism. So the missionaries are on the horns of a dilemma. Should they try to cooperate with the state churches, renew and revive them, and through them reach the unchurched; or should they establish churches of their own? In either case, they have a difficult time. The state churches, by and large, are not open to the American missionaries; and the unchurched people, like the Laodiceans, are "rich, and increased with goods, and have need of nothing" (Rev 3:17).

Missionaries can endure all kinds of hardship and privation if the work prospers and people respond to the gospel; but when the people remain unresponsive, the missionary becomes restive. No amount of creature comforts can compensate for lack of spiritual results. This seems to be the situation in Europe.

Probably the most intriguing part of the study is found in the section titled Classification of Reasons. Why do missionaries become dropouts? The study lists thirty-four reasons, grouped together under three headings: reasons of a personal nature account for 50.6 percent; reasons having to do with the nature of the work account for 25.4 percent; reasons related to social or outside influences account for 24 percent.

The highest single item on the list is physical health, which accounts for 20.3 percent of all missionary dropouts. Mental health is fourth highest with 5.6 percent. Together they account for 25.9 percent of all dropouts. People are constantly asking: Why can't we lower this figure? The answer is that mission boards are doing their best to reduce the dropouts in this and all other categories; but success is difficult to achieve. Missionary candidates have always been obliged to submit to medical tests, and in recent years psychological tests have been added. If serious weaknesses appear in either area, the candidate is usually rejected, unless there is some overriding reason why he should be accepted. But in spite of everything that can be done at this end, physical and mental weaknesses develop after arrival on the field.

One should bear in mind that the wear and tear of life is far greater on the mission field than here at home. Plenty of people in the United States crack up every year, among them not a few Christians. In many countries personal hygiene is unknown and public sanitation is poor or nonexistent. Germ-carrying flies abound on every hand, and parasites by the millions are found in food and water. One glass of unboiled water is sufficient to lay a man low with typhoid fever. Diseases such as smallpox, poliomyelitis, and tuberculosis are endemic in many parts of the mission field. No matter how careful the missionary himself may be, his household servants may completely ignore or forget the instructions they have been given regarding these matters. And if the missionary himself manages to keep out of trouble, what about his children, who spend much of their time in the care of a national? If they fall sick and have to come home, the parents must accompany them. In that case, we have two dropouts, even though neither parent is at fault. When everything is taken into consideration, it is a wonder that the dropouts on account of health are not greater than they are.

The other items under the first category—Reasons of a Personal Nature—are lack of commitment, emotional immaturity, indiscreet conduct, feeling of uselessness, insufficient ability, and marriage. The last named is subdivided into three headings: marriage to a missionary, to a non-missionary, and to a national. Together these three account for 9.7 percent of the total dropouts and call for some explanation.

Marriage to a missionary (2.8 percent) means marriage to a missionary of another mission. Obviously no one is penalized for marrying within his own mission! Strictly speaking, a person who marries into another mission should not be regarded as a dropout, for both partners remain in missionary work. In most cases of this kind, the woman leaves her mission and joins that of her husband. The mission that loses her naturally lists her as a dropout; but she is a dropout only to that mission, not to the missionary cause. Therefore, strictly speaking, she should not be counted as a dropout at all.

Marriage to a non-missionary (6.6 percent) is a different matter. The great majority of these cases involve a single woman missionary who marries a non-missionary. This is a fairly common practice, hence the high percentage of 6.6. The reason for this is obvious. There are three women for every two men in the missionary corps. This means that very few of the single women will ever be able to marry, at least not within missionary ranks. Most women, including missionaries, entertain the hope that one day they will get married and have a family. This is a perfectly natural and legitimate desire.

Some women are able to sublimate this desire and become reconciled to perpetual celibacy. Some even take vows of celibacy. Most women, however, do not; and as they get into their thirties, and life becomes increasingly lonely, the desire for marriage intensifies. When an eligible Christian man comes along and proposes marriage, the reaction is predictable.

The question might be asked: Why does she have to leave the mission? Could not the husband be invited to join the mission? In most cases the man is already established in some business or profession and feels no call to missionary life and work; and even if he did, he may not have the necessary qualifications. If he has the qualifications and desires to do so, there is no reason why both husband and wife should not be members of the mission. Then instead of suffering a dropout the mission would acquire a new recruit. But this is the rare exception.

The third category of marriage is that between a missionary and a national. Through the years most missions have frowned upon mixed marriages. Mission leaders vehemently deny that racial prejudice plays any part in this policy. Rather they point out that the cultural differences between East and West are so great that domestic felicity is difficult to achieve. They also say, not without reason, that unmarried evangelists and Bible women are able to work with single missionaries with a greater degree of freedom and poise if everyone concerned knows that intermarriage is categorically ruled out.

A China missionary married the well-educated daughter of a Chinese pastor. Because he knowingly violated a rule of the mission, he was dismissed. To make matters worse, the parents of the girl publicly disowned their daughter for bringing disgrace on the family by marrying a Westerner. In time children came along to bless the home; but they suffered even more than their parents. Following the evacuation of 1949 this family returned to Scotland. The Chinese wife liked neither the food nor the climate and pined for her parents in far-off China. In school and out, the children were made the victims of racial prejudice. Some ten years later the family moved to Australia, where the father was to teach theology in a Bible college. Two days out of Australia the oldest boy, about twelve years of age, committed suicide in his cabin. Apparently he could not face the ordeal of starting life all over again in the hostile environment of a strange land.

It should be mentioned that both Latin America Mission and Overseas Missionary Fellowship now accept nationals as full members. In this case it is no longer possible to have a rule against miscegenation. Doubtless this is the trend of the future.

Of the twelve items in the section of the study titled "Reasons Having to Do with the Nature of the Work," only two are significantly high on the list: decision to enter homeland position (7 percent) and disagreement with policy (6.9 percent). One wonders if those who accept homeland positions should be reported as dropouts. Most of them remain in what we call full-time, church-related vocations, either with their own mission or with some other Christian organization. Why then should they be listed as dropouts? If a pastor leaves the pulpit in the homeland to accept a teaching position in a seminary, does he thereby become a dropout? Of course not. Then why should his missionary brother be labeled a dropout for doing virtually the same thing? By this definition the author is a dropout, even though he has been teaching missions for twenty years and his students are serving the Lord in all six continents!

Disagreement with policy is a significant item, especially in these days when criticism of the establishment is so vocal and vociferous. It is divided into two parts: disagreement with board policy, and disagreement with field policy. Board and field policy usually do not differ much; but the percentages are significant— 4.3 percent for the former and only 2.65 percent for the latter. Can we learn a lesson here? Board policy is determined in New York, Philadelphia, Wheaton, or Minneapolis. Field policy is made on the field, where missionary participation in policy-making is likely to be greater. Field policy, therefore, is better informed and probably more flexible. Present trends are toward greater decentralization. This is a move in the right direction.

It is comforting to learn that language difficulty and inadequate training account for only .8 percent and .6 percent respectively. This speaks well for the educational institutions that train our prospective missionaries.

The third category is "Reasons Related to Social or Outside Influences." Here the largest number of dropouts is chalked up against incompatibility—7.6 percent. This is broken down into three kinds of incompatibility—with nationals (1.2 percent), with missionaries (2.6 percent), and general (3.8 percent). It is rather interesting to note that missionaries have more trouble adjusting to fellow missionaries than to nationals. One reason for this may be the intimacy of life on the mission field. In the larger centers there is a good deal of institutional work. This is bound to involve a certain amount of communal living, which is always hard on one's sanctification. Missionaries, almost by definition, are aggressive personalities. Living in close quarters, they find it easy to be abrasive. General incompatibility (3.8 percent) is the highest of the three. This is actually equal to the other two combined. This category probably includes those missionaries who don't mix well with anybody, their own kind or somebody else's kind. Overall, incompatibility (7.6 percent) is the third largest cause of missionary failure, after physical health and marriage.

Cultural maladjustment accounts for 2.6 percent. This, though not high, reflects the frequency with which new missionaries fail to adjust to life and work in a cross-cultural situation. No matter how hard we try to "tell it like it is," it is impossible to convey a perfect picture of life in a strange environment. The young missionary must find out for himself; and he doesn't always like what he finds.

Children's health and education account for 3.4 percent and 2.6 percent respectively. Missionaries tend to have large families, and the health and education of the children are major problems for both parents and mission executives. If one of four children in a family becomes chronically ill, the entire family must return home. This means two dropouts (father and mother), not one.

Responsibility for parents claims 3.3 percent of the dropouts. Most of these are single women who feel compelled to remain at home, after three or four terms on the field, to care for aging parents who have no one else to look after them. Sometimes these missionaries are able to resume their work after the parents pass on. Much will depend on the age and health of the missionary when she is set free from family responsibilities.

One other category calls for comment—forced resignations. These account for only .4 percent. This category is the lowest in the long list of thirty-four items. This means that only four out of every 1,000 missionaries have to be dismissed from the mission for all reasons. This is not a bad record.

Contrary to popular opinion, the overall missionary dropout rate is very low. It works out at 14.4 percent at the end of six

years of service! This compares favorably with most other vocations, secular or religious, at home or abroad. When one takes
into consideration all the many factors that militate against the
health and well-being of the missionary, he can only conclude that
the good hand of the Lord must have been upon him during all
these years. If he hasn't been completely immune to the "terror
by night; nor for the arrow that flieth by day," he has certainly
found shelter "under the shadow of the Almighty" (Ps 91:1, 5).
Otherwise the dropouts would have been considerably higher.

Most revealing is a comparison of missionary dropouts with
those of the Peace Corps. The Peace Corps term abroad is only
twenty-one months. Each country is provided with a doctor to
look after the medical needs of the volunteers, and periodic checkups are mandatory. Moreover, the vast majority of the volunteers
are young, therefore less susceptible to illness, and single, therefore without the problems children bring. Even so, the dropout
rate for the Peace Corps is a whopping 17.2 percent over a twenty-
one month period. In contrast, only 2.5 percent of missionary
dropouts occur in the first twenty-one months.

This figure is unbelievably low, but it is borne out by the
statistics of individual missions. Not all missions have the same
dropout rate. Obviously some have a better record than others.
Between 1893 and 1963 the Sudan Interior Mission sent a total of
1,911 missionaries to Africa. During that seventy-year period
total losses, including 76 deaths and 33 retirements, numbered
only 630, or 33 percent. If the losses by death and retirement are
removed, which they should be, then the dropout rate drops to
27 percent. Spread over the seventy-year period, this works out
at approximately .4 percent per year, which is a fantastically good
record.

Or take the New Tribes Mission, much younger than the Sudan
Interior Mission. From 1942, when it began, to 1969, it sent 1,038
missionaries overseas. Of that number, 392 became dropouts, including 20 who died. This represents a 37.8 percent loss over the
twenty-seven-year period. Of the 392 dropouts, however, 71 were
still active in the field in 1969, either independently or in membership with other missions. If these 71 are not counted, the dropout
rate drops to 31 percent for the twenty-seven-year period, which
is slightly more than 1 percent per year—again a remarkably good

record, especially when one remembers that the New Tribes Mission is working exclusively in primitive areas where health services are nonexistent.

The Southern Baptists, with over 2,500 missionaries in more than sixty countries, report an annual dropout rate of only 3 percent for all causes, including death and retirement. Or take the Moody Bible Institute, which began sending its graduates to the mission field before the turn of the century. By 1972 a total of 4,985 Moody alumni had gone to over one hundred countries of the world. Of these, 2,327 were still in active service in 1969. This represents a dropout rate of 53 percent over a period of eighty years. And this figure encompasses all dropouts, including those resulting from death and martyrdom! Missionary Aviation Fellowship, except for two transfers to other missions, did not have a single dropout in the first eighteen years.

If these figures are accurate—and there is no reason to question them—they should forever put to rest the completely unfounded report that "half the missionaries do not return to the field for a second term of service."

When one considers the conditions under which many missionaries have to live—isolation and loneliness, privation and sometimes persecution, enervating climate and inadequate food supply, contagious diseases and epidemics, lack of medical facilities and public sanitation—one marvels that the dropouts are so few.

AN ANALYSIS OF MISSIONARY CASUALTIES

The study was made by the Missionary Research Library of New York. It covered the decade 1953-1962. It included 1409 casualties reported during the decade by 36 boards. These boards included large and small, denominational and faith missions.

The term used in the report is "withdrawals." There are two categories: presumably avoidable withdrawals, and normally anticipated withdrawals. The latter category includes retirements, deaths, short-term missionaries completing contracts, and career missionaries with 20 or more years of service. These four classifications, termed normally anticipated withdrawals, are not regarded as casualties, and, therefore, are not included in the study. Casualties, therefore, include only those who are described as presumably avoidable withdrawals.

BREAKDOWN OF CASUALTIES ACCORDING TO

BOARDS	Missionaries	Casualties
16 large	4,220	1,214
20 small	750	195
36	4,970	1,409

EDUCATION	Number	Percentage
High School	61	4.3
Bible School	403	28.6
College	436	30.9
Seminary	292	20.7
Graduate School	53	3.7
Not given	164	11.6
	1,409	99.8

OCCUPATION	Total Force	Casualties
Evangelistic	35.8%	47.3%
Educational	11.3%	18.0%
Medical	9.4%	14.0%
Other	14.0%	12.0%
Not given	29.5%	8.7%

COUNTRIES	Total Force	Casualties
Africa	26.0%	33.0%
Asia	53.0%	44.0%
Europe	1.5%	2.4%
Latin America	19.5%	17.4%
Not given	—	3.0%

SOURCE: These four charts are from the Missionary Research Library of New York.
NOTE: All figures are as given in original charts.

ANALYSIS OF 1,409 CASUALTIES ACCORDING TO

CATEGORIES	EDUCATION					VOCATION				CONTINENT			
	Bible School 28.6%	College 30.9%	Seminary 20.7%	Grad School 2.7%	Other 1.0%	Evangelism 47.3%	Education 17.9%	Medicine 13.9%	Other 12.0%	Africa 33.0%	Asia 44.3%	Latin Am. 17.7%	Others 5%
Physical Health	18.5%	30.5%	16.6%	9.7%	13.6%	49.0%	16.0%	15.4%	19.6%	48.6%	37.0%	12.2%	1.4%
Psychological Health	10.1%	31.6%	25.3%	3.8%	16.4%	40.5%	15.2%	21.5%	22.8%	40.6%	50.6%	3.8%	5.0%
Lack of Commitment	21.3%	44.6%	10.6%	10.6%	12.7%	42.6%	23.4%	17.0%	17.0%	38.3%	27.6%	32.0%	2.1%
Emotional Immaturity	9.0%	28.4%	19.0%	7.0%	17.6%	43.2%	12.2%	18.9%	25.7%	46.0%	27.0%	21.6%	5.4%
Indiscreet Conduct	41.8%	25.5%	7.3%	5.5%	12.7%	70.9%	10.9%	5.5%	12.7%	38.2%	21.8%	40.0%	—
Disagreement Board Policy	18.3%	18.3%	16.6%	8.3%	21.6%	40.0%	16.7%	11.7%	31.6%	23.3%	43.3%	30.0%	3.4%
Disagreement Field Policy	8.3%	55.5%	8.3%	8.3%	14.0%	66.6%	2.8%	5.5%	25.0%	—	83.3%	11.1%	6.0%
Homeland Positions	17.2%	23.3%	20.2%	15.2%	9.1%	42.4%	21.2%	8.1%	29.3%	20.2%	52.5%	19.2%	8.1%
Incompatibility	13.6%	28.2%	15.5%	12.8%	7.2%	43.6%	22.7%	10.9%	10.0%	33.6%	50.0%	13.6%	2.7%
Family Problems	13.4%	26.8%	16.9%	9.1%	18.3%	43.0%	16.2%	11.3%	29.2%	32.4%	32.4%	16.9%	18.3%

CLASSIFICATION OF REASONS

A. REASONS OF A PERSONAL NATURE 50.6%

   1. Physical health 20.3%
   2. Mental health 5.6%
   3. Lack of commitment 3.3%
   4. Emotional immaturity 5.3%
   5. Indiscreet conduct 3.9%
   6. Feeling of uselessness 2.0%
   7. Insufficient ability 0.5%
   8. Marriage to missionary .... 2.8% ⎫
      Marriage to non-missionary .... 6.6% ⎬ 9.7
      Marriage to national .... 0.3% ⎭

B. REASONS HAVING TO DO WITH THE NATURE OF THE WORK .. 25.4%

   1. Disagreement with board policy 4.3%
   2. Disagreement with field policy 2.6%
   3. Dissatisfaction with work assignment 2.0%
   4. Lack of a sense of accomplishment 0.7%
   5. Language difficulty 0.8%
   6. Inadequate training 0.6%
   7. Decision to enter homeland position 7.0%
   8. Local political disturbance 1.4%
   9. Foreign government restrictions 1.1%
  10. Displacement by nationals 1.2%
  11. Transfer to other church agency 2.5%
  12. Change in work situation 1.2%

C. REASONS RELATED TO SOCIAL OR OUTSIDE INFLUENCES 24.0%

   1. Incompatibility with nationals .... 1.2% ⎫
   2. Incompatibility with missionaries .... 2.6% ⎬ 7.6
   3. General incompatibility .... 3.8% ⎭
   4. Cultural maladjustment 2.6%
   5. Children's health 3.4%
   6. Children's education 2.6%
   7. Responsibility for parents 3.3%
   8. Family problems—economic 0.8%
   9. Forced resignation 0.4%
  10. Negative recommendation from field 1.9%
  11. Change of denomination 0.6%
  12. Not given 0.8%

FOLLOW-THROUGH STUDY OF A CONTROL GROUP
OF WITHDRAWALS

In an effort to gain more depth and precision, we have made a special study of missionaries who were appointed during the first four years of our study. This enabled us to follow through on these appointees from appointment through withdrawal.

We separated from the 1,409 withdrawals under study those appointed between January 1, 1953, and December 31, 1956. From this group those who had served seven or more years were eliminated in order to provide a uniform time span for the four appointed periods (1953, 1954, 1955, 1956). It will be recollected that by the criterion used for the selection of the 1,409, this special study also does not include those who were eliminated due to death, short-term appointments, or unknown addresses. Thus the total loss over the six years is probably slightly higher than intimated here. We find that approximately 85% remained on the field after six years of service. The following table illustrates the withdrawal rate.

| Year | Total No. Appointees | Total No. Withdrawals | No. of Years of Service | | | | | | Percentage of Withdrawal |
			1	2	3	4	5	6	
1953*	524	83	3	12	10	25	24	9	15.6
1954	620	73	3	8	6	16	21	19	12.0
1955	519	80	7	8	10	14	24	17	15.8
1956	520	79	15	7	11	22	15	9	15.1
Totals	2,183	315	28	35	37	77	84	54	14.4**

*Following the 1953 appointees longer, we found that after 9 years, 116, or 22.9% had withdrawn from service.

**Attention should be called to the fact that this is 14.4% of appointees during the four-year period, not of the total active missionary force.

5

WHAT TRAINING IS REQUIRED?

THIS TOPIC is almost as old as the modern missionary movement itself. One of the subjects discussed at the missionary conference in Madras in 1900 was "The Training of Missionaries." In recent decades, especially since World War II, a good deal of consideration has been given to this problem.

There are different kinds of missionaries: long-term, short-term, professional, and nonprofessional. Different missionaries require different kinds of training. In this chapter we are concerned with the training of an elite corps of long-term, professional foreign missionaries. Referring, in reverse order, to the four adjectives used here, they should be defined as follows: (1) foreign, in the sense that they cross geographical and/or cultural boundaries to serve Christ and His church in a country or culture other than their own; (2) professional, in the sense that they feel constrained, after years of preparation, to devote their lives to the service of Christ in some church-related capacity; (3) long-term involves a lifelong commitment to missions in contrast to those who plan to serve for only one term; (4) elite, in the sense that they have been tested in four or five major areas of competence and been found to meet the standards of excellence demanded by the new day.

By using the word *elite* one runs the risk of being censured by some who regard it as their sacred duty to debunk the modern missionary enterprise and reduce the missionary to what they call his "true dimensions." In the past we have acknowledged his superiority; now we are in danger of emphasizing his mediocrity. Ideally he should be above average physically, mentally, and spiritually. In this sense he belongs to an elite corps. If he is not above average, he should think twice before offering for missionary service. There is no place on the mission field for persons who can't make the grade here at home.

In past discussions of missionary preparation we have usually restricted our thinking in two ways. We have ignored the role played by the home and the church and have concentrated on that of the college and seminary. Second, in college and seminary we have been preoccupied with the mechanics of the academic process: the taking of notes and the passing of exams. We have devised tests and measurements whereby we can gauge academic progress, and here we have done a good job. But what about the students' spiritual progress: their growth in grace, their understanding of the will of God, the development of their prayer life, their compassion for the lost, their ability to lead others to Christ, their capacity for enduring hardness as good soldiers of Jesus Christ? Is growth in grace less important than growth in knowledge?

If we are thinking of the educational process simply as the impartation of knowledge, then the school plays a major role, to be sure; but is this not too narrow a view of education?

Christian education is far more than the impartation of knowledge, or even the inculcation of ideas. It is equally concerned with character building, moral standards, value systems; and these are more often caught than taught. Psychologists tell us that the herd instinct runs strong in young people. They tend to take their cue from their peers, not their parents; but this is true only of the less important things in life—the clothes they wear, the songs they sing, the games they play, the books they read. When it comes to the basic things involving ethical practices, moral standards, spiritual values, which determine human behavior, they follow pretty closely the ideas and ideals they imbibe at home.

This being so, it is imperative that missionary training begin at home, that it be maintained consistently and continuously, line upon line and precept upon precept, throughout the years of childhood and adolescence. It is never too soon to begin; it is always too soon to quit. Too often in our day Christian parents neglect their responsibility in this direction. They give their children every advantage that an affluent society affords. They make ample provision for their physical, mental, and social life;

but they do little or nothing to cultivate their spiritual life. They leave that to the church and the Sunday school.

Even those parents who are most vociferous in their profession of the Christian faith deny in deed what they profess in word. And the young people are not slow to detect the discrepancy between what we say and what we do. They take their cue not from what we preach, but from what we practice.

Homes that have no family altar, that do not practice tithing, that never entertain missionaries are hardly likely to produce recruits for the mission field. Parents must themselves be committed to the task of world evangelization before they can influence their children in this direction. Many parents who give generously to the missionary budget of the local church are secretly unhappy when their own children volunteer for missionary service.

And what shall be said about the responsibility of the church? Dr. Harold R. Cook, Director of the Missions Department of the Moody Bible Institute, has expressed the opinion that the church rather than the college is responsible for the paucity of missionary candidates. In spite of all the progress that has been made in the matter of Christian education, there has been very little *missionary* education in the local church.

The average church makes little or no concerted effort to educate the youth in the Christian mission. Even during their Sunday school days they are not required to read a single missionary biography or subscribe to a single missionary periodical. About their only contact with missions comes at the annual missionary conference, and that is rather tenuous.

Most evangelical churches have a missionary conference each year; but seldom is it a learning experience. The messages are usually inspirational, not educational. Moreover, the young people are seldom involved. They have no representatives on the missionary committee; hence they have no part in the planning of the conference. Certainly they are not expected to have a vital part in the program. Rightly or wrongly, they feel that the missionary conference is of the adults, by the adults, and for the adults. The highlight of the conference is not a call for young people to dedicate their lives to missionary service, but an appeal for the adults to increase their faith promise. If that goes over the top, all is well; the conference has been a success. Usually the young people are out in full force to only one meeting—the Sunday morning service. A few will return for the evening service. Probably none will be present during the week. It is possible for a missionary conference to come and go without making any lasting mark on the youth of the congregation.

What about the pulpit ministry? Does the average pastor in our evangelical churches make a significant contribution to the missionary cause? How often does he preach a missionary sermon? How much does he personally know about missions? Is he really interested in missions or is he chiefly concerned with the housekeeping chores of the local church?

If our young people have not acquired an interest in missions during the ten or twelve years they have been attending church, why should they suddenly manifest concern for missions when they reach college? By that time they have made up their minds that missionary work is not for them. The college, instead of being able to build on the foundation laid by the church, must start all over again to arouse interest in the cause of missions. In the meantime, the church has missed a unique opportunity.

So much for the informal preparation in home and church. What about college and seminary?

Fifty years ago a missionary could get away with a high school education. That is not true today. Educational standards are rising, not only in the United States but all over the world. Several factors, most of them new in this postwar period, are responsible for this: (1) the acquisition of national sovereignty, which now permits the newly independent nations of the world to determine their own destiny, (2) a universal passion for learning, which has resulted in a rapid spread of literacy and the upgrading of educational standards in all parts of the Third World, (3) the resurgence of the great ethnic religions of the Orient, which presents the Christian missionary with an unprecedented challenge, (4) the worldwide apparatus of Communist propaganda, which portrays Uncle Sam as the Goliath of Western imperialism and the missionary body as the spearhead of cultural aggression, (5) a state of ferment, intellectual, political, economic, and social, which is slowly but surely rising to the point where it will boil over in what

Adlai Stevenson called a "revolution of rising expectations" which will upset the status quo in Asia, Africa, and Latin America.

In these exciting days of exploding nationalism and expanding knowledge, the missionary candidate deserves the finest education offered by an up-to-date, well-rounded curriculum taught by competent personnel with first-hand knowledge and experience.

Missionary preparation is not as simple as it once was. The missionary movement of our time is a vast, worldwide enterprise offering an almost endless variety of opportunities and demanding an equal number of skills. Those going into such technical branches of missionary work as radio, aviation, and medicine will require specialized training. It does not require a knowledge of Hebrew and Greek, or even of church history, to operate an airplane over the jungles of New Guinea. It does require highly developed skills not usually obtainable in a theological seminary. To further complicate the situation, we now have long-term and short-term missionaries. Obviously, short-termers can get away with less preparation than long-termers under certain conditions. This being so, it is no longer possible to lay down rigid guidelines when it comes to academic programs for prospective missionaries. Much will depend on the country to which they will go and the kind of work in which they will engage.

If a man is going to teach college or seminary in India or Japan, he should have one or two advanced degrees. On the other hand, if he expects to spend his life among a primitive people with no education at all, he will be an intellectual giant with only a high school education. And there are, as we know, some missions that are called of God to work exclusively among such people. We should not, then, be too critical of the low academic standards accepted by these missions. For the time being, and perhaps for some years to come, there will be a place for such missions. Their candidates may not need advanced degrees, but they will require knowledge and skills not offered by most colleges in this country. It then becomes the responsibility of the mission to provide the special training demanded by the situation. Colleges and seminaries cannot be expected to offer that kind of training.

The United States government follows this policy in its Peace Corps program. The volunteers spend some weeks on a university campus in a very intensive academic program. Following this they spend several weeks in boot camp, living and working under conditions which approximate those of the host countries. Among the missions, Wycliffe Bible Translators and New Tribes Mission follow this procedure, providing their own jungle and boot camps. In these camps the program is highly specialized and tailored to the needs of life in the jungle.

For most missionaries a broad base in the liberal arts is no longer a luxury; it is a necessity. The frontiers of human knowledge are being pushed back at an alarming rate, so that excellence today may be mediocrity tomorrow. The world is shrinking so fast and human knowledge is increasing so rapidly that today's missionary candidate should get all the education he possibly can. Only so will he be able to cope with the intellectual, social, political, and religious problems he is likely to encounter in the course of his ministry. This is especially true if he plans to work among students or other intellectuals, and more and more missionaries are doing just that.

The missionary candidate will find some liberal arts subjects of more value than others, depending on his sphere of service and the caliber of the people served. The philosophy major will find his discipline of immense value in the Far East, of considerably less value in Africa, and of little or no value in New Guinea.

It would be a trifle difficult to discuss Plato's *Republic* or Aristotle's *Metaphysics* with the Stone Age savages of the Baleim Valley. On the other hand, the anthropology major will find his discipline to be extremely relevant to the Indians of the Amazon, less relevant to the Arabs of the Near East, and almost irrelevant to his cousins in Western Europe.

History is another excellent major for the missionary candidate. In these days of sudden cataclysmic change, the missionary especially needs the balanced perspective that comes from an understanding of the historical process. He will be more patient with the fledgling governments of Africa and Asia if he has read American history candidly and critically without rose-tinted spectacles. We too had our ups and downs. We made our share of blunders. We produced our crop of demagogues, some of them of recent vintage. Our political structure almost came apart on more than one occasion. The student of history will bear these facts in mind and avoid the errors and arrogance of some American journalists, who cannot refer to certain African and Asian leaders except in derogatory terms.

Nor should the study of history be limited to American or European history. Equally important is the history of the Middle East, Asia, and Latin America, to say nothing of African history. The unprecedented upheaval in Red China in the past two decades, and her pathological hate for the West in general and Uncle Sam in particular, can be understood only in the light of nineteenth-century history in that part of the world. It is a regrettable fact that the Christian college, with its comparatively small student body, its correspondingly small faculty, and its very restricted budget, is not able to offer the wide range of subjects taught in the Ivy League schools and the state universities.

Communications in general, and journalism in particular, offer tremendous potential for the modern missionary. With the new nations devoting in some instances more than 50 percent of the national budget to education, it is difficult to overstate the value of journalism in the literature program of present-day missions.

In a world seething with social ferment and plagued with political instability, the study of political science is of enormous practical value. It is important that today's missionary not only be acquainted with his own political institutions, but also have some knowledge of the history and strategy of colonialism, nationalism, and Communism. He will then realize that none of these is to be condemned completely, that all of them have good points as well as bad. Many ex-China missionaries have lamented the fact that back in 1949 when the Communists came to power they didn't know what it was all about. Few of them had ever read a single book on Communism.

It should be observed in passing that certain limitations mar our teaching of philosophy, history, and literature. By philosophy we really mean Western philosophy. Oriental philosophy is considered to be little better than mythology. Likewise, our literature courses are usually restricted to American and European works. Until recent years our textbooks on world civilization completely ignored everything east of the Khyber Pass. To call this world civilization is just another evidence of our ethnocentrism.

In addition to a broad base in the liberal arts, missionary candidates should have a good theological education. The best place to acquire this, of course, is in a theological seminary, where three full years are given to the study of the Bible, theology, church history, apologetics, Hebrew, Greek, Christian education, and pastoral studies. This is a must for all missionaries going into evangelistic work, church planting, or Bible teaching. Those who cannot afford three years in seminary should have at least a one-year concentrated Bible course. The Bible schools have done yeoman service in this area. Many of them continue to make a significant contribution.

The missionary candidate, however, needs more than liberal arts and theological studies. He should have the equivalent of at least one year of professional studies. To enter the teaching profession here at home one must have a major in education. To work for Dupont or General Electric, one must have a degree in science or math. But to become a professional missionary, one can dabble in anything! At least, this seems to be the prevailing notion in many circles. This kind of thinking is fallacious. It is naïve in the extreme to imagine that a single course in general psychology will enable a person to understand the Oriental mind, or that a study in American sociology will enable one to understand and appreciate such exotic cultures as are found in Asia, Africa, and many parts of Latin America.

Most seminaries as now constituted are not equipped to give this kind of professional training. The program is designed for the pastor at home, not for the missionary going abroad. The time has come for theological educators to face up to the special needs of the student preparing for service on the foreign field, and to restructure the seminary program to include subjects that are indispensable to the missionary candidate. This will mean drastic changes. We must either extend the course from three years to four or revamp the three-year program to allow for the vocational subjects which are so necessary. Here, of course, we run into prejudices, priorities, preferences, vested interests, administrative red tape, and a host of other problems. What department head is willing to eliminate one of his courses to make room for a course in missionary anthropology? Winston Churchill was not the only man who was reluctant to preside over the liquidation of his own empire! Theologians, no less than politicians, have blind spots. They cling tenaciously to the status quo and fight change.

If we really believe that world evangelization is the mission of the church, then every theological seminary should have two programs: one for the person going into the pastorate here at home, and another for the person looking forward to work on the mission field. There will, of course, be much common ground in the two programs, perhaps as much as two full years. But every seminary program should include a core of twenty or thirty semester hours of mission subjects for the benefit of the students heading for the mission field. These courses could be concentrated in the third year or scattered throughout all three years of the seminary program.

What are some of these courses? Linguistics is extremely helpful for anyone who wants to learn to read, write, and speak a foreign language accurately and fluently after he has become an adult. If he gets into translation work, especially the kind that involves primitive languages never before reduced to writing, linguistics is a must.

For anyone expecting to serve in an alien culture, missionary anthropology is indispensable. One of the greatest mistakes of the nineteenth century was the average missionary's failure to appreciate things foreign, be they customs, cultures, values, or virtues. They were "strange" and therefore inferior. Anthropology more than any other discipline will help to correct the superiority complex which has been characteristic of the Western world. It will also afford the missionary a healthy degree of relativism. We could hope, however, that anthropology be taught by Christian professors, for anthropology taught within a purely naturalistic, humanistic framework can do as much harm as good. The secular anthropologist takes a dim view of the missionary enterprise and openly frowns on any attempt to convert people from one religion to another.

Another very important subject is area studies. It is an act of consummate folly to go to Africa or Asia, whose cultures are so different from our own, without a fairly adequate knowledge of their history, culture, and religion. Carlos Romulo, one-time foreign minister of the Philippines, writing in the *Asian Student*, January 27, 1957, had this to say:

> It makes little difference whether the penguins of Antarctica know anything about the squirrels of Rock Creek Park. But it

makes all the difference in the world whether the American people understand the crowded millions who inhabit Asia. Your destiny, Asia's destiny, the world's very survival, may depend on such an understanding on your part.

If this is true of Americans in general, how much more is it true of those Americans who live and work abroad? In spite of this warning from one who knows, thousands of Americans go abroad every year with little or no orientation: the catastrophic results are vividly documented in *The Ugly American.*[1]

At least one course should be devoted to a comprehensive study of the country in which the candidate will be working. This should include geography, history, economics, politics, religion, Christian missions, and the indigenous church. With such a course under his belt, the young missionary will arrive in Nairobi, Tokyo, or Caracas with a working knowledge of the people and the land of his adoption. In times past many a missionary landed on the field to find himself a babe in the woods. If area studies are to be worthwhile, a school of missions should have one full-time faculty member from each of the four major cultural areas of the world: Asia, Africa, Latin America, and the Muslim world.

For decades Harvard, Stanford, and Yale universities have offered courses in non-Western studies, but only in the past thirty years have similar courses been introduced into other colleges. By 1964 American universities offered 153 programs on the graduate level and 23 programs on the undergraduate level. Almost 150 foreign languages, most of them modern, are now offered in American colleges. It seems that at long last Americans have discovered that there are six continents as well as seven seas in the world.

There are those who see no need for such a specialized subject as history of missions. Charles R. Taber suggests that such a course is "essentially rootless and remedial." He claims that church history, if properly taught, would include history of missions.[2] Maybe so; but until now it has, apparently, not been properly taught, Traditionally church history has been preoccu-

---

1. William J. Lederer and Eugene Burdick, *The Ugly American* (New York: Fawcett, 1963).
2. Charles R. Taber, "The Training of Missionaries," *Practical Anthropology* 14 (1967):268-69.

pied with councils, constitutions, schisms, crusades, papal bulls, royal patronage, denominational rivalry, ecclesiastical structures, religious wars, controversy, heresy, and apostasy. Some thought has been given to the development of the Christian faith and the building up of the Christian church; but very little attention has been devoted to the spread of the gospel and the conversion of the heathen world. And until it is, we must continue to teach the history of the Christian mission as a separate subject. It is rather strange that the history of the Christian mission, the most glorious chapter of all, should be omitted from the history of the church.

It goes without saying that the missionary candidate should have a working knowledge of the non-Christian religions. Here again, it is an act of folly for the missionary to attempt to work in a Buddhist country with no knowledge of the history, sacred books, or major doctrines of that religion. The minimum requirement should be a survey of the major religions. In addition it is well to take an in-depth course in the major religion of the country or area to which the missionary expects to go. Missionaries to Africa should understand animism, and those who go to Asia should be familiar with one or other of the great ethnic religions: Hinduism, Buddhism, Confucianism, Shinto, and Islam.

Cross-cultural communications, rather new to the seminary curriculum, is another valuable course. If it is difficult for the theologian and preacher to communicate the gospel to the modern American, who shares both his culture and his religion, how much more difficult is it to communicate the Christian gospel to men of other faiths. No less a theologian than Paul Tillich was obliged to confess that one of the most decisive events of his life was his visit to Japan, where a face-to-face confrontation with Buddhism introduced him to a new world of thought.

Ecumenics is another pertinent subject. Without doubt the ecumenical movement is the most dynamic force in institutional Christianity in the twentieth century. What began on the mission field in the nineteenth century as a rivulet has become a mighty river whose swift-moving current threatens to carry everything before it. No missionary can afford to be ignorant of this phenomenon. He should understand both its strengths and its weaknesses.

When the missionary candidate has completed his seminary

training, he is still not ready for the mission field. If at all possible, he should take a pastorate for a year or two, or attend Missionary Internship for nine months. This will afford an opportunity to test the theories, principles, and techniques he learned in school. There he will learn that adults, like children, do not always respond according to the book. He will discover that the theories propounded in the solitude of the ivory tower do not always work out in the hurly-burly of the world arena; that principles that look good on paper do not always apply to people. He will gain experience; he will acquire patience; he will become more flexible. He will learn to roll with the punches, to adjust to persons as well as events, to improvise; yes, and even to compromise.

Like all beginners he will make mistakes; but they are better made at home than on the mission field. He will find an assistant pastorate in a large city church, under the sympathetic eye of a competent senior minister, to be of great value. On the other hand, he may find a rural church or a small-town church closer to the conditions he will encounter on the field. In either case, he will learn lessons that will stand him in good stead for the rest of his life.

Now the young man is ready for candidate school. That, too, is part of his training. Candidate school has a twofold purpose: to enable the mission to gain a thorough knowledge of the candidate, including his character, temperament, idiosyncrasies, strong points, and weak points, and to determine as accurately as possible his chances of success; and to permit the candidate to become thoroughly acquainted with the inner workings of the mission, its personnel, principles, policies, finances, doctrines, and distinctives. No questions should be barred. No information should be withheld. The candidate has as much right to know the mission as the mission has to know him. He should be allowed to ask any question he considers pertinent.

Answers should be full, honest, accurate, and frank. Some mission executives become impatient when the young candidate asks about retirement benefits. The question is perfectly legitimate. It may be a trifle premature from the chronological point of view, but this does not, or should not, rule it out.

It is to the advantage of the mission to lay all its cards on the table and let the candidate make up his mind in the light of all the facts. If he is to be disillusioned with the mission, it had better come in candidate school than on the field. It will save a good deal of money and not a little heartache.

It is very important that the young missionary have proper supervision and counsel during his first term on the field. Every effort should be made to help him over this exceedingly difficult period. If he spends a year or so in language school with other expatriates, his encounter with culture shock will be much more gradual and much less traumatic; but sooner or later the full confrontation will come. It is important that during this period he have the sympathy and support of the mission personnel.

Three questions are important. Where will he go? What will he do? Who will be his senior missionaries? The wrong answer to any of these questions may well spell the difference between failure and success.

Where will he go? If possible he should go first to a station or a city where he will get a favorable impression of missionary work and church life. To place him in the most barren station in the mission could easily break his heart and send him home. He should get off to a good start in a good location.

What will he do? Until he becomes fluent in the language he will not be able to do much; but from the beginning he should be given something to do. Whatever it is, it should be something for which he is equipped, something in which he has an interest, something in which he can take pride. This will help to keep him from frustration.

Who will be his senior missionaries? They should be chosen with great care. Not everyone is cut out by gift or temperament for the role of senior missionary. They may be wonderful people, good teachers, fine administrators, and hard workers. If they don't know how to handle other people, especially inexperienced young missionaries, who need a lot of TLC during those first years, they should not be asked to take young workers under their wing. Many seasoned missionaries, some old and some not so old, have long since become inured to the hardships of missionary life and work, and they forget what culture shock meant to them ten or twenty years before. Quite unconsciously they put a yoke on the neck of the young missionary which neither they nor their predecessors at that stage were able to bear. Try as he may, the young worker cannot keep up. By and by he becomes weary in well doing and may easily become a casualty.

There are those who suggest that the national church should share responsibility for the pastoral care of the young missionary. Several articles on this subject have appeared in *International Review of Mission*. Where church and mission are integrated this would, doubtless, be a normal procedure and could prove helpful. In other situations much would depend on the strength of the church and the maturity of its leaders. Certainly the first-term missionary is a missionary in the making, and it will be some time before the process is complete.

The last stage of the missionary's training coincides with his first furlough. This is an excellent opportunity to put the capstone on his long period of training. He has been on the field for three, four, or five years. He has learned many things, including his own deficiencies in certain areas. He may want to make up these deficiencies. Or he may have discovered a new area of interest which necessitates further training to permit him to function effectively. In either case, furlough provides the opportunity to improve his usefulness in his second term of service. Furlough was designed in the first place to provide not only recuperation from the past but also preparation for the future.

College graduates looking forward to teaching in their second term may want to obtain teacher certification. Persons with only a baccalaureate degree may want to work towards a master's degree. Some with only a master's degree may wish to do more advanced study. Those who went to the field with only a liberal arts education and little or no Bible and theology could well spend the year of furlough in seminary or Bible college. Seminary graduates, on the other hand, may want to brush up on vocational or professional subjects. Others may feel the need of area studies at one of the state universities. Fuller Seminary, Trinity Evangelical Divinity School, and other seminaries now have a School of World Mission. An increasing number of missionaries on furlough profit from studying in these institutions.

Mission executives should encourage their younger missionaries to spend at least part of their first furlough in an academic institution where the climate is conducive to thought and study, and the facilities are adequate for research and writing. One or two semesters in such an environment, apart altogether from the knowledge gained, would act as a mighty stimulant to heart and mind and send the missionary back to the field renewed in vision and vigor.

Two things are important here. If at all possible, the mission should provide financial aid to cover the cost of tuition, books, and other fees and should extend the furlough period if necessary to enable the missionary to complete his program. It should also set him free, at least during the academic year, from deputation responsibilities. This will require the sanction of the mission and the understanding of the constituency. The churches that support him should be contacted by the mission, the study program explained, and their sympathy and support solicited. Some missionaries on furlough carry a full academic load and engage in deputation work on the side. After a weekend that involves hundreds of miles of car travel and three or four services, they return to the campus thoroughly exhausted just in time for their Monday morning class. Wednesday evening they are off to another meeting. This is grossly unfair to the missionary. Every effort should be made by the mission to conserve the strength of the missionary so that he can give his undivided time and thought to the pursuit of his studies.

In spite of all the "Yankee Go Home" slogans on the billboards of the world, missionaries are still needed and still wanted by the indigenous churches overseas. Almost to a man their leaders are asking for more and better missionaries. We dare not disappoint them. We must see to it that missionary candidates are given the very best training—academic, theological, and vocational—that our institutions of higher learning can afford.

6

THE NEW MISSIONARY FOR THE NEW DAY

FEW PROBLEMS in modern missions are greater than that which relates to the role of the missionary in this post-colonial period. World War II marked the beginning of the end of the colonial structure. First in Asia and later in Africa, the colonies demanded and received their independence. When the United Nations was founded in 1945, there were 51 charter members. Today the member states number 132. All the countries of Asia are now politically independent. In the great continent of Africa over forty new nations have been born since Ghana led the way in 1957. Only two large colonies remain, Angola and Mozambique. Both belong to Portugal. France still has the Territory of the Afars and the Issas on the horn of Africa. Rhodesia and South Africa have serious internal problems; but at least the states are independent, although a majority of the peoples are hardly free.

The collapse of the worldwide colonial structure in this postwar period has had enormous effects on the missionary movement. For better or worse, the missionary movement of the nineteenth century formed an integral part of the colonial thrust into Asia and Africa. Nineteenth century colonialism had three phases: political, economic, and cultural. The diplomat represented the first, the merchant the second, and the missionary the third. Indeed the missionary, more than the diplomat and the merchant, was responsible for the rise and spread of nationalism.

Had it not been for the missionary with his liberating gospel and his educational institutions, not a single country in Black Africa would be free today. It was the missionary who reduced over 400 languages and dialects to writing, and then taught the

African to read his own language. It was the missionary who opened schools—tens of thousands of them—and provided free education for the Christians and non-Christians alike, thereby opening the African mind to the whole world of books, from Plato's *Republic* to Lincoln's Gettysburg address. Above all, it was the missionary who gave the most explosive, most liberating book in the world, the Bible, to the people of Africa; and he gave it to them in their own tongue. It was the missionary who by precept and example inculcated the ideals of democracy, including the dignity of man, the worth of the individual, and the freedom of the human spirit. Today there is hardly a leader in Black Africa who is not the product of a mission school, Protestant or Roman Catholic.

The great missionary movement of the nineteenth and twentieth centuries has passed through three stages. During the first period the mission was the dominant organization, and the missionary was the master. During the second period church and mission cooperated, and the missionary was the partner. In this postcolonial period, the church is the dominant organization, and the missionary is the servant. This is not an easy role to play.

Existing Situation in the New Day

In all but a few mission fields the missionary is still needed by the church. We hear a good deal about the indigenous church in all parts of the world, and many persons jump to the conclusion that missionaries are no longer needed. The indigenous church is there, all right, and we rejoice in its presence and progress. Indeed, we should blush with shame if we had to confess that after almost two hundred years of blood, toil, and tears, we had not produced a church that can stand on its own feet. These indigenous churches are often referred to as being self-governing, self-propagating, and self-supporting. All of this is true; but we should understand exactly what is meant by these expressions. Some churches are self-supporting only in the sense that no foreign funds are used to support the program; but if the truth were known, there is little to support. Other churches which are listed as self-governing depend heavily on subsidies from the West. No church is truly independent if a major part of its program is dependent on outside help.

And even if all these overseas churches were truly and completely independent, could they be expected to complete the evangelization of their own countries without outside help? Many of them are woefully weak numerically, financially, and in other ways as well. All the Protestants in India combined represent only about 1 percent of the population of 550 million. All the Protestants in Japan number about half a million, out of a total of 105 million. All the Protestants in Mexico represent about 3 percent of the population of fifty million. Is it realistic to suppose that these numerically weak churches can finish the job of world evangelization without help?

What about finances? Here the churches are even weaker. In most of the countries of the Third World, the average per capita income is between one and two hundred dollars per year. Beverley Nichols in his book, *Verdict on India*,[1] says that the Indians are so poor they can live on the smell of an oil rag! This is obviously an exaggeration; but maybe we need this kind of overstatement to drive home to the affluent people of the West the unbelievable poverty of the Third World. After one hundred years the Methodist churches in India are still unable to fully support their own pastors. The Baptist churches have the same problem. The great Church of South India, the largest in the country, continues to receive substantial sums of money from the supporting missions. If the Indian churches cannot scrape together enough funds to support their own pastors, how can they raise enough funds to support Bible schools, theological seminaries, and Bible societies, to say nothing of educational and medical institutions?

It is still too soon to quit. If we quit now, we may be in danger of losing everything. The missionary is still needed. No one recognizes this better than the churches themselves.

In all but a few mission fields the foreign missionary is still wanted by the church. There may be places where for political reasons it is wise for the church to dissociate itself from the West. This is obviously the case in Communist countries. Nationalism is running high in some countries and the churches are being pressed by their governments to free themselves of all entangling alliances

1. London: Jonathan Cape, 1944.

with the West. The situation vis-à-vis the American missionaries is further aggravated by the cold war, which continues unabated in many parts of Africa and Asia and is beginning to manifest itself in Latin America, where revolution is a way of life.

There may even be church leaders in some of these countries who, for reasons of their own, resent the presence and prestige of foreign missionaries; but certainly they would represent a small minority. The vast majority of churches and church leaders in the Third World, if completely free of government pressure, would wish to retain the services of the missionary. They want to have a say in the kind of missionary they receive; but they are not prepared to go it alone at this stage.

In 1960, the year that saw seventeen countries get their independence, Bishop Lesslie Newbigin made an extensive tour of Africa. He was surprised to find widespread support for continued missionary presence. He found repeated emphasis on the need for the missionary to be wholly a part of the church in Africa. Patterns of life and administration which make a separation between "church" and "mission," which keep certain things exclusively in the hands of a group of missionaries, which treat the mission as merely a temporary scaffolding to be removed when the church is built—all these were strongly condemned by African leaders. But equally strong was the desire to have the continued fellowship of missionaries from the West who would be in the African church as salt in meat. Over and over again the national leaders that he contacted had specified, "Send us missionaries who will be one with us, live with us, work with us, die with us, and lay their bones with ours in Africa."[1]

Mission boards should ascertain the wishes of the national churches before assigning missionaries to them. If the churches are self-governing, as we say they are, then they should be consulted before new missionaries are sent to them. It is very easy for mission leaders to pay lip service to the concept of the autonomy of the indigenous church and at the same time be guilty of "backseat driving." It is not enough that we take our hands off the wheel. We must be careful not to give orders from the back seat! In a sense, back-seat driving is often more offensive than front-

1. *World Mission Newsletter*, January 1961.

seat driving. The latter is open and acknowledged by all; the former is a subterfuge.

The emphasis should be on quality rather than numbers. The tendency in mission circles is to emphasize the lateness of the hour, the greatness of the harvest, and the paucity of workers. The cry is for "more workers," and one gets the impression that the task can be accomplished if we only get enough laborers into the vineyard.

Fifty years ago missionaries with a Bible school education were able to do a commendable job; and in some primitive areas of the mission field they still have a contribution to make. But with rising standards of education all over the world, a three-year Bible course is hardly sufficient to meet the demands of the new day. Today's missionary must be able to hold his own with the new class of intellectual elite found in all the large cities of the Third World.

By quality, however, we don't mean only intellectual acumen, but spiritual prowess as well. In recent years there has been a concerted effort to downgrade the missionary, to persuade the home constituency that he is not the spiritual giant he was thought to be in the nineteenth century. Students returning from a summer on the mission field tell us that their greatest discovery was the fact that "missionaries are human beings." It is but a step from this to the conclusion that today's missionary is just like any other Christian in the homeland, no better, no worse.

There is always the danger of going to extremes. Doubtless it was a mistake to regard the nineteenth-century missionary as a hero. Perhaps he was not as spiritual as his supporters considered him to be. But today we seem to have gone to the opposite extreme. We are telling ourselves that consecration is not a matter of geography and that an ocean voyage or a plane trip doesn't make anyone a saint. All of this is perfectly true, and the missionary himself would be the first to deplore his own lack of spirituality. On the other hand, are we suggesting that modern missionary service does not demand a higher degree of sanctification and dedication than is found in the *average* church member at home?

The national churches on the mission field are no longer prepared to accept any Tom, Dick, or Harry that we choose to send them. They don't want ecclesiastical or administrative leaders. Certainly they don't want armchair strategists. But they do want spiritual leaders. They want leaders who will be an example to the flock and will exemplify in life and character the virtues they seek to inculcate in others. They want men they can love and trust, men of integrity, sincerity and humility. They want men in whom they can readily discern the love of Christ and the fruit of the Spirit. They want men who are spiritually mature as well as theologically sound; men who know what it is to live a life of prayer, to walk by faith and not by sight; men who can eat bitterness without turning sour, endure hardness without becoming callous; men who can go the second mile and stay on the job after the sun has gone down. They want men who are modest in their wants and simple in their tastes, who can live happily without all the accoutrements of Western civilization. They want men who are willing to identify with them in good times and bad, men who will work and play with them, laugh and weep with them, feast and fast with them. They want men with a full measure of faith, hope, and love. In a word, they want men of God. It is a thousand pities that seminary training in the West is weighted predominantly in favor of the preparation of the mind, with little thought or time given to the cultivation of the spiritual life.

Missionaries should be willing to serve under the national church. The missionary began in the nineteenth century as a master. Later, as the indigenous church began to emerge, his role changed to that of a partner. Now he is called upon to go one step farther and become a servant. He has always regarded himself as a servant of Christ—nothing very difficult about that. Now he must become a servant of the church. This is neither easy nor pleasant. But it is the way the Master went, and we as His disciples must follow in His steps.

Jesus Christ was and is the Master. But in the incarnation He became the Servant. He came, as He said, "not to be ministered unto, but to minister" (Mt 20:28). He was first of all the Servant of Jehovah. In this capacity He took His cue from His Heavenly Father. Both His words (Jn 12:48-50) and His works (Jn 5:19) were ordered and ordained by His Father. Indeed, it was His meat to do His Father's will (Jn 4:34). "Though he were a Son, yet learned he obedience by the things which he suffered" (Heb 5:8). Even He did not find servanthood particularly easy.

But more than that, His role as Servant extended to his relationship to the disciples. "I am among you as he that serveth" (Lk 22:27). To drive home the point, at the Last Supper he stooped to wash their feet; and, lest they miss the point, he added, "If I then, your Lord and Master, have washed your feet; ye also ought to wash one another's feet" (Jn 13:14).

Throughout its long history the church has not taken kindly to the practice of footwashing—literally or figuratively. From time to time small groups have made a practice of it; but even they are careful not to overdo it. Usually it is a once-a-year ritual. To be quite truthful, footwashing is not particularly attractive, unless, of course, the feet belong to us! Not many people are lining up for the privilege of washing the other fellow's feet. By nature we much prefer to be master. Only as the grace of God becomes operative in our hearts will we deliberately choose servanthood.

The supreme test of the modern missionary movement may well lie right here. Are we willing to be servants, not just of the Lord, *but also of the church?* Do we have the humility required to esteem others better than ourselves (Phil 2:3)? Are we prepared to take the lowly place and play second fiddle to those with less skill and experience than ourselves?

Missionaries will be acceptable to the national church only if they can produce. Time was when the national church was happy to receive any missionary simply because he was white and enjoyed a certain degree of prestige. That day is gone. Now the missionary must prove himself. It is not enough to be sincere, kind, loving, and humble. He must have some gift, some skill, something to contribute to the life and work of the national church. Every believer has been given at least one gift by the Spirit. Presumably the missionary has had an opportunity to cultivate his gifts to the point where they are apparent to himself and his peers in the Christian community. Otherwise, he had better remain at home for a few more years until his gifts have been sufficiently developed to enable him to make a tangible contribution to the national church when he reaches the mission field.

Many boards now evaluate the missionary's life and work at the end of each term of service. Those with a poor record are not invited to return to the field. This is a step in the right direction. If a man is a misfit on the mission field, he ought to know it and take steps to remedy the situation. However in most cases the decision is now made by the board. Has the time not come to invite the national church to help in the work of evaluation? After all, the mission exists for the church, not the church for the mission. If the missionary is serving with the national church, it seems only reasonable that the church should be given a voice in this important matter.

Some ask, "Will this not jeopardize the status of the missionary?" There is no reason to assume that it will. Other things being equal, church and mission are not likely to differ widely on a given missionary. If the mission senses that he should not return overseas, it is safe to assume that the church will concur in the judgment. On the other hand, the view of the church might serve to support the status of the missionary. Conceivably the national church might go to bat for a missionary whose service has been called in question by the mission. So it works both ways. In any case, if we are to do more than pay lip service to the autonomy of the national church, we must consult its leaders when missionary service is under review.

DIFFICULTIES IN THE NEW DAY

It would be naïve to imagine that the new situation created by the emergence of a fully autonomous national church does not pose any new problems. We had problems under the old regime. We shall have problems under the new. It seems only right and proper that some of the problems be brought out into the open and discussed in an atmosphere of candor and coolness.

Church leaders may succumb to pride and mistreat the missionary. Nationalism is a very potent force in international relations. It is still a strong influence in the Christian church. Now that missionaries are servants of the national church, its leaders may wish to assert their authority as soon as possible. They might very well test the good intentions of the missionary by asking him to accept a disagreeable assignment. If he knuckles down and reacts with good grace, the church leaders might change his assignment. If, however, his reaction is one of resentment or rebellion, it will only confirm their suspicion that he was not really prepared to accept the authority of the national church.

Worse still, the church leaders, remembering the days when the missionaries mistreated them, might very well use their new-found authority to the discomfort of the missionary. The desire for revenge is one of the strongest impulses of human nature. Now that the national church has come into its own, some of its leaders might want to "settle old scores." However, the possibility is rather remote. Most nationalists, political and religious, have been most magnanimous in their treatment of their erstwhile masters. Indeed, it is surprising the amount of goodwill there is in Africa and Asia toward the former overlords, Britain, France, Belgium, and Holland. Certainly Christian leaders are not behind political leaders in this respect.

Church leaders might not make the best use of the missionary. In educational circles in the West there is an increasing emphasis on specialization, with the result that many missionaries today are specialists of one kind or another. Naturally when they get to the field, their chief concern is to get into the kind of work for which their training has prepared them. Nobody wants to be a square peg in a round hole. The more training and experience a person has, the more irksome such a situation becomes. Few experiences are more frustrating.

If the assignment is a *pro tem* arrangement, the missionary can be expected to live with it; but if it turns out to be a permanent position, he is likely to be unhappy. No man can do his best over a long period of time unless he is genuinely happy in his vocation. It is imperative, therefore, that the well-qualified missionary be assigned to the kind of work that will best utilize the training he has acquired. Otherwise, he is likely to be lost to the mission field. Church leaders are not so apt as mission leaders to be aware of this problem; and because of this they might easily make the assignment on the basis of need rather than of training. They may assume that the missionary, by his very dedication, is willing to be all things to all men in order to get the job done. All unwittingly they may assign him to a task for which he has neither the gifts nor the training.

Church leaders may discriminate against the missionary. In every vocation there are posts that are attractive and others that are less attractive. This is particularly true in those parts of the world where mental and manual labor are divided into two distinct compartments. Throughout the Orient, wherever Confucianism has been an influence, society is neatly divided into two main classes, those who work with their hands and those who work with their minds. Teachers, authors, scholars, musicians, artists, and preachers belong to the intelligentsia. In China they all belonged to the *hsien-seng* class, until the Communists turned the world upside down. To the literati, manual labor was degrading. No scholar would demean himself by driving his own car or cutting his own lawn. There were "laborers" for that kind of work.

In this kind of situation the missionary, without any such inhibitions, is a very convenient fellow to have around. To him all labor is the same. He then becomes the logical choice for the menial tasks which are so distasteful to the nationals. In countries where the churches are more advanced, some missionaries find themselves driving cars, operating equipment, and repairing machines, while the most prestigious positions are filled by nationals.

If the missionary is especially trained for these tasks and feels happy with them, there is no reason why he should not make his contribution in this way. But if these jobs are assigned to him because they are distasteful to the nationals, then the missionary may feel that he is the victim of discrimination.

Church leaders may be reluctant to replace the missionary. The aim of missionary work is to establish a truly indigenous church which can stand on its own feet, manage its own affairs, train its own clergy, and pay its own way. Sooner or later, preferably sooner, the missionary ought to work himself out of a job. But when the time comes for the church to assume full responsibility for its own affairs, it may be reluctant to replace the missionary with a national. After all, the missionary represents something for nothing, a gift to the church by the mission that continues to pay his salary. As a rule the mission supports the missionary, not the office which he holds. When the missionary terminates his service and the office passes to a national, the mission subsidy ceases. This being so, the national church will think twice before suggesting that the missionary be replaced by one of its own.

The problem is basically an economic one. Most churches on the mission field are desperately poor by Western standards. If they can pay their local pastors a living wage, they are doing well. To take on the support of a high office previously held by a missionary is beyond the financial strength of many churches. Under such circumstances it is only natural that the church leaders should continue to hold on to the missionary even when they have a qualified national to take his place. Where this is done the growth and development of the church are bound to suffer.

Church leaders might lose their vision for evangelism. One of the greatest dangers of church-mission merger is the death of evangelism as a vital part of the church's outreach. As long as the mission is in charge, evangelism is likely to be assigned high priority; but when control passes to the national church and the missionaries are under its direction, all too often evangelism is allowed to lag. The church leaders become so engrossed in church affairs and administrative duties that they forget the prime mission of the church—evangelism. The missionaries under their direction are assigned to housekeeping chores in the many institutions now under their care.

In some parts of the world, where the old-line denominations have a large investment in foreign missions, there may be seventy-five or one hundred missionaries in a given country, and not one of them engaged in evangelism. The missionaries are pretty well confined to institutional work. The local churches, in charge of national pastors, are content to maintain their own existence with little or no concern for the spiritual needs of the non-Christian population all around them. In many instances the church members are second- and third-generation Christians whose profession of Christianity may be cultural and traditional, rather than personal and vital. Because they have left their first love, evangelism is no longer a live option. They are imprisoned in a ghetto of their own making, and seldom do they sally forth to do battle with the world, the flesh, or the devil. They make practically no impact on the pagan world around them. Their only growth is biological, and even that is small. After a visit to Brazil, Howard

A. Johnson, an American Episcopal rector, remarked, "Such growth as we can show is due, for the most part, to the fact that Brazilian Episcopalians have children."[2]

When the missionary finds himself in this kind of situation what is he to do? In former days, when the mission was in charge, the missionary could call for a change in policy; but now that the church is independent and the missionary serves under its direction, he can only make suggestions. Under these conditions the missionary who is dedicated to the proposition that all men are lost, and that only through hearing and believing the gospel can they be saved, will find his missionary experience a very frustrating one.

Where There Is No Church

It stands to reason that the missionary can serve under the national church only where such a church exists and where the church is willing to cooperate in the evangelization of its own country. It should be borne in mind that there are some countries without an organized church, in other countries the national church is a persecuted minority whose chief problem is one of survival, and in still others the church has become so moribund that it has no interest in evangelism. In such circumstances the missionary will have to be prepared to go it alone.

Sad to relate, there are second- and third-generation churches on the mission field that have developed a "ghetto" complex and consequently are concerned solely with their own existence. They have no missionary vision at all. It would be fruitless for the missionary to try to work with that kind of church. Such a decadent church does not have the right to tell the missionary what he may or may not do. At all times the missionary must be free to fulfill the Great Commission as he understands it—with or without the approval of the national church.

Moreover, one of the exciting developments in recent years is the emergence of missionary organizations in the Third World. Some are denominational. Others are interdenominational. Still others are international. These groups are prepared to train, send out, and support their own missionaries. Most of these missionaries now are going to other parts of the Third World, but the

2. Howard A. Johnson, *Global Odyssey* (New York: Harper & Row, 1963), p. 42.

time may come when they will help to evangelize the West. And why not? Too long have we subscribed to the notion that world evangelization is the "white man's burden." The time has come to fully internationalize the missionary movement of our day. In recent years several Western missions have opened their membership to non-Caucasians. Before the end of the century, we may find Western missionaries serving under Asian, African, and Latin American boards. That will truly be "joint action in mission."

CHARACTERISTICS OF THE NEW MISSIONARY

It goes without saying that the new day calls for a new kind of missionary. It does not require much sanctification to be a master or even a partner; but it requires an enormous amount of grace to be a servant. More than ever before, modern missionaries will have to be "wise as serpents, and as harmless as doves" (Mt 10:16). In addition to all the character traits of the past, he will have to acquire some new ones.

He will have to be humble. Humility is one of the outstanding virtues of the Christian life. According to Philippians 2, it lies at the heart of the incarnation. Jesus Christ not only became man, but as a man He humbled Himself and took the form of a servant. To His disciples He said, "Take my yoke upon you, and learn of me; for I am meek and lowly in heart: and ye shall find rest unto your souls" (Mt 11:29). Even with the teaching and example of Christ before them, the apostles failed to learn the lesson of humility. After three years in the company of the Master, they argued among themselves as to who was the greatest. Even our Lord had difficulty inculcating the virtue of humility in His apostles.

In former days when the missionary was the master, there was little need for humility. That quality was shown by the nationals. But now the missionary is the servant. Will he be able to fill the role with ease and poise? Not without a good deal of humility. Of course, there is nothing new about humility. We have always preached humility to others. Now it is our turn to exercise it.

He will have to be patient. The average missionary is not very patient. In fact, Westerners as a group are not known for their patience. Patience seems to be an Oriental virtue. We in the

West are apt to be activists. We are in a hurry. We want success, and we want it in the shortest possible time. We have instant tea, instant coffee, and now instant lawns. We can't bear to wait for the seed to germinate. The long-drawn-out process from seed to sprout, from sprout to stock is much too slow. We want the harvest in a hurry.

When the missionary arrives in the Third World, he finds himself in an entirely different climate. Life is much more leisurely. Business, government, transportation, even the military, move at a much slower pace. The Christian church is no exception. It too moves forward gradually, cautiously, haltingly, much to the exasperation of the missionary. Somehow the missionary will have to learn to slow down. The church cannot be expected to follow the missionary in his mad rush against time. The missionary will have to fall in step with the church. To adjust from the jet plane to the ox cart will require much patience.

There is another area that will call for patience. Once the national church is in complete control of its own affairs, it is bound to introduce changes. Most leaders, including missionaries, tend to resent changes introduced by their successors. The old ways, they say, were better. But change is bound to come. The missionary must be prepared to trust the Holy Spirit to direct and control the national church and not fret or pout when it decides to develop new patterns and policies more in keeping with its cultural heritage. More than that, he must be willing for the national church to make mistakes. Some changes will not necessarily be for the good of the church; but the missionary will have to be patient and allow the church leaders to learn by their mistakes. The missionaries made their mistakes and lived with them. The church leaders should have the same privilege.

He will have to be tactful. Tact is the ability to do and say the right thing in the right way at the right time. This kind of skill is important in one's own culture. It is absolutely invaluable in cross-cultural, interracial situations. At the heart of the Confucian ethic is the concept of *lee*—propriety. On one occasion Confucius said to his disciples, *Ruh Ching Wen Yu,* which being interpreted means "Upon entering a territory inquire about its customs." That is why the Chinese, from time immemorial, have been past masters at the delicate art of interpersonal relations.

In contrast we Westerners tend to be direct and abrupt in both speech and manner. We consider it our duty to tell it like it is and let the chips fall where they will. We pride ourselves on our honesty and integrity, and insist that everything must be open and aboveboard. We are suspicious of anything that smacks of flattery or rhetoric. In our dealings with others we don't want a third party to interfere. We dislike favoritism. We eschew patronage (except the politicians, that is). We abhor nepotism. We wear our hearts on our sleeves and don't care how many times we lose face. We prefer candor to courtesy and prudence to propriety. Little wonder that we have so much trouble in dealing with our brethren overseas!

In the days when the missionary was the master, his rough and ready manners had to be endured by the nationals. But now that they are in positions of authority, the missionary, as the servant, will have to acquire a certain degree of tact. It is not enough to speak the truth, it must be spoken in love. It is not enough to do the right thing, it must be done in the right way. No matter how clever we are, we might not be able to settle our differences without the counsel of a middleman.

If the missionary is going to fill the role of the servant with grace, he will need the meekness of Moses, the patience of Job, and the tact of Barnabas.

7

THE PEACE CORPS VERSUS THE CHRISTIAN MISSION

THE PEACE CORPS got under way in the early months of the Kennedy administration. The first contingent of volunteers arrived in Ghana in 1961. Since then the Peace Corps has sponsored over 40,000 volunteers in some sixty countries of the world.

When President Kennedy first announced the formation of the Peace Corps, there were many skeptics. Richard Nixon attacked it during the 1960 presidential campaign. President Eisenhower described it as a "juvenile experiment." The *Wall Street Journal* opposed it as a "Children's Crusade." The *Richmond New Leader* termed it a "cheap substitute for true patriotism." The *Philadelphia Inquirer* called it a "staggering example of John F. Kennedy's loose thinking." In some quarters it was referred to as the "Kiddie Corps."

As usual, the critics overstated their case and lived to rue the day. As things turned out, the Peace Corps has achieved a fair degree of success, so much so that many other countries, including Canada, Germany, Japan, and Israel, have instituted their own version of the Peace Corps. In spite of its weaknesses and failures, the Peace Corps has been one of the few bright spots in our whole foreign aid program. Certainly at the grass roots, it has done more than any other agency of the government to create goodwill and understanding between the United States and the host countries.

According to President Kennedy, the threefold objective of the Peace Corps was (1) to provide interested countries with qualified volunteers to help meet their needs for trained manpower, (2) to help other peoples understand America better, (3) to help Americans understand other peoples better.

Neither the ideals nor the methods of the Peace Corps were new. Both were based on previous experience gained from the modern missionary movement and the International Volunteer Service, founded in 1953.

The Peace Corps and the Christian mission have much in common. The qualifications for service are parallel in many areas. Applicants for the Peace Corps must have attained their eighteenth birthday. If married, husband and wife must apply together, be assignable together, and live together during their term of service. The Peace Corps is more lenient than the Christian mission in matters pertaining to health. Health requirements are stated in negative rather than positive terms. The applicant must have no disqualifying medical or physical condition, such as tuberculosis, venereal disease, or other infections. Physical handicaps, such as blindness, diabetes, asthma, or a crippled limb, are no deterrent. Likewise there should be no evidence of mental or emotional disturbance. Academic qualifications are flexible. One does not have to be a college graduate. In fact, about 50 percent of the Peace Corps volunteers have no degrees at all. The number of missionary candidates with college degrees is considerably higher—maybe as high as 75 percent. The Peace Corps volunteer must, of course, be an American citizen. Each volunteer is expected to have a special skill. Nothing is said about spiritual qualifications. Indeed, religion is definitely played down. More than one applicant has been rejected because he took his religion too seriously.

Both the Peace Corps and the Christian mission require a period of orientation at home before going abroad. For the Peace Corps volunteers there is a thirteen-week period of intensive training. Over 125 colleges and universities have cooperated in providing facilities and professors for the program. Language study looms large and consumes about half the entire time. Some time is spent acquiring or improving a skill. Other studies include American history and politics, and the culture of the host country.

Missionary candidates also have an orientation period which usually lasts anywhere from ten days to three weeks. During this time the mission seeks to introduce the candidate to the history, methods, and philosophy of the mission and give him some idea of what he can expect when he reaches the field. Language study is almost always postponed until arrival on the field, where it is acquired with greater speed and accuracy. No attempt is made to teach history or politics. It is assumed that the candidate has had these subjects in college. Missionary candidates who have majored in missions in college or seminary are the best prepared for service overseas and require little or no additional training in candidate school.

In the Peace Corps the rate of attrition before reaching the field is rather high. Only a fraction of those who initially apply ever serve overseas. There are no reliable comparable statistics for missionaries; but it is safe to assume that here too the rate of attrition is high.

How do the Peace Corps projects compare with those of the Christian mission? The Peace Corps has three hundred projects which are divided into four major categories: education, community development, agricultural extension, and public health. Missionary work, as traditionally defined, has been divided into five categories: evangelism and church planting, education, medical, technical, and humanitarian work. Through the years the missionaries have engaged in most of the projects now attracting the attention of the Peace Corps.

The main difference between the Peace Corps and the Christian mission is that missionary work is religious in character and content, whereas religion plays no part at all in the operations of the Peace Corps. The latter ministers to the mental and physical needs of the individual and the social and economic well-being of the community; whereas the missionary enterprise endeavors to minister to the needs of the whole man—body, mind, and soul.

One half of all Peace Corps volunteers are engaged in education. The remainder are divided almost equally among the other three categories. Among the missionaries, evangelism and church planting claim the largest number—about 35 percent.

It is instructive to compare the personnel of the two groups. In the Peace Corps the men outnumber the women three to two. In the Christian mission the reverse is true; the women outnumber the men three to two. In the early years of the Peace Corps only one volunteer in ten was married. Later the figure rose to one in five. The volunteers are permitted to marry; but if the wife becomes pregnant, the couple may have to resign. In the beginning couples with children were rejected; but that has been changed. The vast majority of volunteers are single. They range in age from eighteen to eighty.

In the Christian mission nearly all the men are married. Inasmuch as the women outnumber the men three to two, many women missionaries remain in single blessedness. Most of these single women fare amazingly well. In the Christian mission, at least the Protestant branch of it, the average family has three or four children. Their health, education, and general well-being constitute a perennial problem.

Remuneration is always an important factor. How do the Peace Corps and the Christian mission compare in this area? The volunteer is the only American abroad whose remuneration approximates that of the missionary. The volunteer receives a salary of $75 a month, which is kept at home and given to him upon his return. His overseas living allowance varies from country to country, but it usually works out at about $100 per month. The Peace Corps volunteer is required to live with and like the people among whom he serves. He is not allowed to own his own car or bicycle. He is expected to use public transportation—second and third class where available.

The missionaries, while not exactly rich, have maintained a higher standard of living than the volunteers. They live in better houses, may own a car, and have more of the amenities of our mechanical civilization. With few exceptions they have not been able to identify with the people as closely as the Peace Corps volunteers. This is partly due to the fact that most missionaries are married and have small children living at home; care must be taken to protect them from contamination and disease.

On the whole the Peace Corps operation is more costly per capita than is the missionary enterprise. Much depends, of course, on how one reckons; but if we take the total number of volunteers and divide them into the total Peace Corps budget, we find that it costs $13,750 per year per volunteer. Using the same method of computation for the Christian mission, it costs approximately $9,000 per year to maintain each missionary. This includes everything—overhead and administrative services at home and overseas.

The missionary figure looks even better when we recall that the missionary enterprise is much bigger and older than the Peace

Corps. Also, the Peace Corps has no investments whatever in land, buildings, vehicles, and equipment overseas; whereas the missionary enterprise maintains thousands of institutions, large and small, in well over one hundred countries of the world. When all this is borne in mind, it is evident that the Christian mission operates much more economically than does the Peace Corps. This hardly comes as a revelation. The United States government has never been known to operate as efficiently as private enterprise.

The overseas experiences of the two groups are surprisingly similar. To begin with, both experience culture shock. The Peace Corps speaks of three periods of depression through which the volunteer goes. The first occurs when he arrives in the host country. One corpsman wrote from a remote village in the Philippines:

> This is the hardest thing I've ever done. Absolutely nothing is familiar and I often feel totally alone. The physical difficulties actually help, as they take my mind off myself and the feeling of suddenly being cut off from the rest of the world. You cannot imagine the gulf between East and West, and it makes me laugh now to think that I expected to bridge it with a smile and a handshake.[1]

The second period of depression usually occurs about the third or fourth month, after the glamor has worn off and the worker settles down to a humdrum existence. Another corpsman wrote:

> I live in a picturesque bamboo mat house I built myself. I buy my water from a picturesque boy with a burro loaded down with water cans. I read and write under a kerosene lantern, sleep on a cot, and cook on a camp stove. There comes a day when all this suddenly becomes no longer picturesque, no longer quaint, but furiously frustrating; and you want like crazy just to get out of there, to go home. This is called "culture shock." It happens to one and all, usually about the third or fourth month.[2]

The third period of depression coincides with the reentry into stateside culture. After finally adjusting to the "strange" culture of the host country, the volunteer must face the ordeal of read-

---

1. Quoted by Roy Hoopes, *The Complete Peace Corps Guide* (New York: Dell Pub., 1966), p. 179.
2. Ibid., p. 187.

justing to the American way of life. Returning to his native land is not an unmitigated pleasure. It has its sorrows and regrets.

The volunteer returns with a different perspective on life in general and the American scene in particular. He seems to react sharply to what he considers shortcomings in American society—commercialism, racism, provincialism, conformity, and the immaturity of his own generation. Just as the poverty of the host country rose up and smote him in the face when he went out, so the affluence of America pains him on his return. In the place of want he finds waste; in the place of frugality there is prodigality. Happiness there consisted in the simplicity of one's wants; here it consists in the multiplicity of one's possessions. It takes time to make the adjustment.

All of this is quite familiar to the missionary. He too knows what culture shock is. He has his times of discouragement and depression. Sometimes he too wishes he had purchased a return ticket. He feels the loneliness and the isolation, and often longs for the sights and sounds of home. And when he returns to the homeland, he too finds it difficult to adjust to the old way of life. Somehow things have changed. Or is it he who has changed? Of course he enjoys clean, efficient service stations, the fabulous supermarkets, the four-lane highways, to say nothing of Howard Johnson's twenty-eight flavors of ice cream. But in the midst of all the wealth and waste, he feels just a little out of place. He has lived with ignorance, poverty, and disease, and he can never be quite the same again.

How does the Peace Corps compare with the Christian mission in the matter of personal self-fulfillment? When it was first launched, the Peace Corps enjoyed enormous popularity. Doubtless some of this was due to its association with President Kennedy. Some of his charisma rubbed off on the new enterprise. In the early sixties it caught the imagination of the younger generation. College students and others flocked to the banners. At one time applications were being received at the rate of five thousand a month.

Almost overnight the Peace Corps volunteer became a hero. There was hardly a reputable magazine in the whole country that did not feature at least one article on the Peace Corps. A Peace Corps *Bibliography* prepared in June 1969 lists no fewer than

44 books and 294 articles on the Peace Corps. *Newsweek* and *Time* led the list with 22 articles each.

When the volunteers left home, they were given a gala send-off. While they were away, the hometown newspaper carried articles and pictures of the local boy serving a noble cause in some far-off corner of the world. Upon his return, he was feasted and feted and given a hero's welcome. Few ventures in American history have commanded such widespread support or received such universal acclaim.

In stark contrast to all this is the Christian missionary. Once upon a time he too was a hero; but not now. His halo has slipped; his image is badly tarnished. As far as the news media are concerned, he comes and goes unnoticed, unless, of course, he happens to get killed. When he leaves for distant parts, only his closest friends are there to see him off. When he returns five years later, there are neither banners nor bugles to herald the event.

But all is not well with the Peace Corps. It too is beginning to lose its glamor. As early as 1965 Franklin H. Williams, U.S. Representative to the United Nations Economic and Social Council, addressed ninety Peace Corps trainees at Brown University. In the course of his address he said: "You're not pioneers anymore. The glamor is gone. If you expect now to be viewed as a hero or heroine when you return, you're mistaken."[3]

Applications are falling off, making it necessary to spend thousands of dollars to recruit new volunteers. During 1967, recruitment on a national scale dropped 30 percent. G. D. Berreman, writing in *Nation*, February 26, 1968, called the Peace Corps "A Dream Betrayed," and described the once glamorous crusade as "moral imperialism."[4] Much of the disenchantment with the Peace Corps in recent years is a reflection of the country's increasing disillusionment with the Vietnam War. Be that as it may, it would seem that the Peace Corps has fallen on evil days. In January 1972, Congress slashed its budget, resulting in drastic cutbacks in personnel from eight thousand to four thousand and in the number of host countries from fifty-five to forty. If this trend continues, the Peace Corps in a few years may be fighting for its life.

3. Ibid.
4. Gerald D. Berreman, "A Dream Betrayed," *Nation* 206 (February 26, 1968):263-68.

What kind of reception has the Peace Corps received in the host countries, and what has been the measure of success?

Over the past eleven years the Peace Corps has worked in some sixty countries with gratifying results. Wherever the volunteers have gone, they have been well received by government officials, students, merchants, peasants, and children. The Peace Corps goes only where it is invited; and it expects the host government to cooperate actively in all aspects of its program. The policy of the Peace Corps dictates that national counterparts be assigned to work alongside the Peace Corps volunteers. In this way the corpsman has a companion and the national receives training. The Peace Corps will not initiate any programs of its own, nor is it permitted to provide materials or funds for the projects undertaken. That is the responsibility of the host government. The purpose of the Peace Corps is to help the people help themselves.

Fifty percent of all volunteers are engaged in education. From many points of view this is the most rewarding of the four categories into which the Peace Corps is divided. The educational worker can arrive one day and begin teaching the next. He does not have to wait for some program to be developed. Immediately he takes his place on the staff of an existing institution. The program is already in progress; all he has to do is fit into the existing structure. The class is a captive audience, waiting almost breathlessly to hear his first words of wisdom. The morale among the educational corpsmen has been consistently high, and not without reason.

The corpsmen deployed in the other three categories of work have not fared so well. Their lot has not been an easy one. This is especially true of the person engaged in community development. His plan of operation is as follows. First he moves into a village, finds himself a place to live, and proceeds to make friends with the people. This may take anywhere from three weeks to three months, depending on the circumstances. Second, he studies the situation and decides what he thinks is the most pressing need in the community. It may be a one-room schoolhouse, a public bath, a children's playground, a well, a road, a bridge, or any one of a hundred other projects. Third, he must sell his project to the people of the village, and he must do it in a democratic manner designed to teach these simple folks the advantages of the democratic process as practiced in the United States.

The local people may or may not buy his bill of goods. If they turn him down, there is nothing he can do but start all over again on another project. That too may be rejected. At this point the volunteer is likely to experience his full share of frustration. He thought the people would surely see their need once it was pointed out to them; but not so. It was not long before the Peace Corps discovered that its three great enemies are ignorance, suspicion, and indifference; and the greatest of these is indifference.

In this respect the Peace Corps and the Christian mission have much in common. Missionaries too have found that ignorance and indifference are enormous obstacles to overcome. A missionary engaged in medical work in the Gorkha district of Nepal wrote to friends:

> It is a humbling experience to come into an area of half a million people served by one other missionary doctor and realize that 90 percent of the inhabitants couldn't have cared less whether we came or not. Most of the people here still have not come to appreciate any particular advantage in modern medicine. In their view we are simply another kind of peddler selling our wares. They regard us with a natural distrust and suspicion, not being able to comprehend our motive for coming to their land. . . . Many of our patients have no sense of gratitude for our services; rather they expect that we be grateful to them for providing us with an opportunity to gain merit for ourselves by treating their illnesses.

> Perhaps the greatest obstacle to improving health care in an area such as ours occurs in the field of preventive medicine. Centuries old customs and superstitions militate against any hope of significantly improved health standards until widespread and effective health education can be made available to the younger generation. We are looked upon with amusement when we fuss about all sorts of invisible creatures like bacteria and tiny worms. Nepalis prepare and serve their meals on mud floors and eat with their hands. Their water supply is usually contaminated, and they resist boiling their water because it flattens the taste and uses up their already limited firewood. Latrines and outhouses are a curiosity, and the progressive citizen who ventures

to construct such a facility usually abandons the whole project after a week because the place stinks so badly.

The numerical strength and geographical spread of the Peace Corps is considerably smaller than that of the Christian mission. The former is now working in fifty-five countries of the world, whereas Christian missionaries are found in twice that number of countries. The number of Peace Corps volunteers now stands at 8,000, whereas the total number of American Protestant missionaries is about 33,000.

The Christian mission has not engaged in as many different kinds of projects as the Peace Corps; but it has ministered to the basic needs of the whole man—body, mind, and soul. It was there long before the Peace Corps was conceived, and will doubtless remain long after the Peace Corps has ceased to exist.

The Peace Corps has not invested in land or buildings, nor has it established any permanent institutions. In contrast, the Christian mission has established tens of thousands of churches, schools, hospitals, and other institutions in all parts of the world.

Some of the finest institutions in the Third World have been missionary enterprises. In China, Protestant mission boards established and maintained thirteen full-fledged Christian universities. Hundreds of institutions of higher learning were established in India and Japan. It is difficult to exaggerate the influence of the American University of Beirut, which has served the intellectual needs of the people of the Middle East for over one hundred years.

The same is true of the many medical institutions established throughout the world by Christian missionaries. The latest *Directory of Protestant Medical Missions* lists a grand total of 786 general hospitals, 565 dispensaries, and 33 sanitariums, served by 1,379 national doctors and 883 missionary doctors.[5] Figures for Roman Catholic medical institutions would be comparable.

One of the outstanding institutions is the Christian Medical College and Hospital, Vellore, India, founded by Dr. Ida Scudder, who began her work in 1900. Her first school building was a vacant shed. Her original equipment consisted of two books, a microscope, and a few bones! On its staff today are 385 full-time

5. Arthur W. March, comp., *Directory of Protestant Medical Missions* (New York: Missionary Research Library, 1959), p. 91.

doctors, 436 graduate nurses and 223 paramedical workers. In training are 337 medical students, 329 nursing students, and 158 postgraduate students.[6]

What about morale in the Peace Corps? On the whole it has been high, especially in the early years. More recently there are signs that it is sagging. Dissatisfaction has been expressed with some of the rules, particularly the prohibition against owning motor vehicles. Complaints have been lodged against the meager salary of $75 a month. Not a few volunteers have been unhappy with their assignments. Particularly galling has been their inability to get their assignments changed.

We have heard much in recent years about dropouts among missionaries, and a whole chapter in this book is devoted to that problem. What is not so well known is that the casualty rate in the Peace Corps is much higher than that among missionaries.

The entire January-February, 1970, issue of the *Peace Corps Volunteer* was devoted to a discussion of "Extensions and Early Terminations." Between 1961 and June, 1969 a total of 39,389 volunteers served under the Peace Corps. Of these, 6,769 terminated their service before the end of the two-year period. This represents 17.2 percent. The picture, however, is not all dark. For every two persons who terminated prematurely, one person decided to sign up for a second term of one or two years. The region with the best record was East Asia and the Pacific, where the number of extendees just about equalled the number of dropouts.[7]

The motivation for a second term of service, however, was not the highest. One volunteer, herself an extendee, writing from Malaysia, said:

> Volunteers generally extend here because we have such a good life, not because of job or Peace Corps-related ideas. The climate is delightful year round, the food is plentiful and delicious, the people usually gracious and friendly, the standard of living one of the highest in Asia. English is widespread and the chances for travel to diverse countries and cultures are excellent.[8]

6. *Vellore News*, Spring-Summer 1972, back cover.
7. "'Why I'm Leaving' 'Why I'm Staying,'" *Peace Corps Volunteer* 8 (January-February 1970):2-3.
8. Ibid.

How are we to explain the large number of early terminations? There are many contributing factors, but the most frequent is frustration, much of which is due to the ignorance and indifference of the people. This, however, is not the whole story. In the Peace Corps, as in the Armed Forces, there is not a little bureaucracy; and this tends to dampen the spirits of the volunteers. The volunteer quoted above went on to say:

> Volunteers leave early, including 20 percent of my group, because of poor, inconsistent, incomplete planning by Peace Corps and the local government. Many jobs, mine included, and most counterparts are fictional and our pleas for better placement and follow-through have not gotten results.[9]

The critical comments of the corpsmen are instructive. Bill Dionne, who worked in Nepal, said, "Why am I leaving? Yesterday had been quite pleasant. Tomorrow was good to look forward to. But the present, the moment now, became unbearable."[10]

After six months in Ecuador, Richard Farinto confessed: "I find myself deeper and deeper in a hole of doubt, bitterness, irresponsibility, and utter confusion."[11] Another wrote:

> The escalating tensions and frustrations of living in a totalitarian state, combined with those of enforced idleness, have finally become intolerable for me. Even the taunting cries of "foreigner" and the stones thrown by small children, which in better days I could easily rationalize or ignore, have begun to take effect.[12]

Pretty Christine Jacobson taught seventeen English classes each week in the town of Arak, Iran. Try as she might, she was not able to feel at home in Muslim society. She stuck it out as long as she could. When she determined to be herself, she left Iran. Her explanation: "I'm tired of role-playing."[13]

Missionaries too have been unable to stick it out. Many of them

9. Ibid.
10. Bill Dionne, " 'The Present Is Unbearable,' " *Peace Corps Volunteer* 8 (January-February 1970):5.
11. Richard Farinto, " 'Deeper and Deeper in a Hole of Doubt,' " *Peace Corps Volunteer* 8 (January-February 1970):7.
12. " 'Tension, Idleness Intolerable for Me,' " *Peace Corps Volunteer* 8 (January-February 1970):6-7.
13. Christine Jacobson, " 'I'm Tired of Role-playing,' " *Peace Corps Volunteer* 8, nos. 1-2 (January-February 1970):9.

have terminated their service in the middle of a term, and others
have failed to return after furlough. It is only fair to say, however,
that the casualty rate among missionaries is considerably lower
than that of the Peace Corps. The missionary dropout rate is 2.5
percent for the first two years; the Peace Corps rate is 17.2 percent
for the same period.

The Peace Corps takes good care of its volunteers. They are
not placed in worksites where health hazards are so great that real
dangers are posed. In the host countries the volunteers are at all
times under the care of U.S. Public Health Service doctors
charged with the specific task of providing medical care for them.
Volunteers are rarely more than a few hours away from competent medical service; and they are visited regularly by the medical staff. Living conditions vary from country to country, but are
usually better than the volunteers expected. They generally live
in modest but adequate quarters, often sharing a rented house
or apartment with other volunteers.

How has the Peace Corps fared in these difficult times when
"Yankee Go Home" is plastered across the billboards of the
world? Some countries, such as Japan, made it quite clear that
they had no need for the Peace Corps. Other countries who
needed the Peace Corps expressed no desire for its services. In
some instances the politics of the cold war had something to do
with the decision. But some sixty countries in Africa, Asia, Latin
America, the Middle East, and the Pacific Southwest requested
and received Peace Corps volunteers. The vast majority of these
countries have expressed satisfaction with the performance of the
corpsmen, asking for additional volunteers year after year.

Peace Corps policy demands that the volunteers keep out of the
internal politics of the host countries. This they have been careful
to do. However, they have engaged in demonstrations against
America's involvement in Vietnam, to the embarrassment of the
United States government and the government of the host country. A rather delicate situation developed in the spring of 1970
when Vice President Spiro Agnew visited Afghanistan. At the
last minute sane counsels prevailed and the anti-war demonstra-
tion was called off. But in spite of their efforts to remain aloof
from internal politics, they have not escaped the vicissitudes of
political life in several of the host countries. As a result, the

Peace Corps has been expelled from half a dozen countries in as many years.

The expulsion from Indonesia was the result of Communist pressure in the days when President Sukarno was flirting with Red China. In Libya the expulsion followed a palace coup engineered by a leftist military junta in 1969. In September of that year the government of Malawi passed a resolution asking for the withdrawal of the Peace Corps due to complaints by the people about the unhealthy influence that the Peace Corps volunteers had over their children because of bad behavior and slovenliness. In the case of Somalia, no explanation was given. Other countries from which the Peace Corps has withdrawn include Gabon, Tanzania, and Pakistan.

It is rather interesting that when the Peace Corps was expelled from these countries, the Christian missionaries were permitted to remain. Does this mean that the missionaries, once regarded as the spearhead of "cultural imperialism," are now accepted for what they are—representatives of the church and not the state? It would seem so. More than one African head of state has publicly expressed his confidence in the missionaries and thanked them for the contribution they have made to the achievement of independence. When Jomo Kenyatta came to power, he asked the missionaries to remain and help build a new Kenya.

One question remains. Should a dedicated Christian desirous of working overseas serve with the Peace Corps or sign up with a mission board? The answer is a simple one. He should do whatever the Lord wants him to do. Obviously not every Christian is expected to serve overseas; and not every Christian serving overseas should do so as a missionary. The Lord needs His servants in all walks of life here at home. Presumably the same thing holds for overseas. Hundreds of dedicated Christians have served with the Peace Corps and have greatly benefited by their experience. Not a few of these have since returned to the field as missionaries. So it is not an either/or proposition. Before a young Christian settles for the Peace Corps rather than the Christian mission, however, certain considerations should be borne in mind.

First, the Peace Corps is not as glamorous as it once was. Already, after one decade, its image is somewhat tarnished. We are living in a fast-moving world in which both men and movements lose their appeal in no time at all. The going has been hard. The problems have been massive. The overall, long-term results have been disappointing. Much of the idealism still remains, but it takes more than idealism to solve the enormous problems of the Third World.

Second, life in the Peace Corps is not as exciting as most people have been led to believe. Most of the problems that have vexed missionaries through the years have plagued the volunteers also. In addition, the Peace Corps volunteers have had to live with a type of bureaucracy virtually unknown in missionary circles. They also have had to secure the cooperation of the government of the host countries, and this has been a perennial source of irritation; whereas the missionaries have worked in cooperation with the national churches.

Third, contrary to popular opinion, the Peace Corps volunteer is expected to accept a degree of regimentation comparable to, if not exceeding, that of the missionary. Hundreds of Christian youth are "turned off" because of what they believe to be the inflexibility of the mission boards, with their outmoded rules and regulations. But the truth is that the Peace Corps has its rules and regulations and these are enforced with equal rigidity. It is difficult for a corpsman to get the Peace Corps to change his assignment; most mission boards do their best to see that the missionary is happy with his assignment. If not, he will be transferred to another place or different job.

Fourth, the Peace Corps is a thoroughly secular operation. It is concerned solely with the physical, material, intellectual, and social needs of mankind. It has only one dimension—the horizontal. The vertical dimension is entirely missing. On the contrary, the missionary enterprise is based on the conviction that man does not live by bread alone. He needs bread, to be sure; but he has other needs as well. He is body, mind, and soul; and if he is to develop a well-integrated personality and live a full-orbed life, the spiritual part of his nature must be cultivated.

This does not mean that the Peace Corps volunteer cannot bear a quiet and effective witness for Jesus Christ as he goes about his work; but it does mean that he is practically prohibited from making any kind of contribution to the building up of the Christian church in the host country. Why should a Christian doctor prefer to serve under the Peace Corps, with its purely secular approach to life, while hundreds of mission hospitals in all parts of the world are crying out for qualified medical personnel? Anyone —Jew, Gentile, Christian—can join the Peace Corps; but only dedicated Christians can serve with the Christian mission. In a word, the missionary can do anything the volunteer does; but the volunteer cannot do everything the missionary does.

Fifth, in most parts of the Third World the Christian church is a woefully weak and feeble institution. In the whole of Asia, where half the world's population lives, only 2.5 percent of the people are professing Christians; and that includes Roman Catholic, Eastern Orthodox, and Protestant believers. In some large countries the total Protestant community is less than 1 percent of the population! It goes without saying that the church in all these countries can stand all the help it can get. It is particularly hard pressed for qualified personnel in its many medical and educational institutions.

There are missionary doctors who cannot come home on furlough and others who cannot retire at sixty-five years of age because there is no one to take their place. In some places there is only one missionary doctor (and no national doctors) for two or three hospitals. Some hospitals are closed and the drugs are gathering dust on the shelves, not because the government cracked down on missionary work, but because there are no qualified personnel to keep the institution open. Five years ago a mission hospital in Thailand installed a dental clinic with all the latest equipment. To date the clinic has not been used. In spite of repeated calls for a missionary dentist, even on a short-term basis, no one has volunteered. During this time hundreds of dentists have served with the Peace Corps. Church leaders in the Third World can be forgiven if they look with envious eyes on the Christians in the Peace Corps.

Sixth, the Peace Corps is a short-term operation. Twenty-one months and it's all over. That's barely time to become acculturated. It is possible for the volunteer to sign up for an additional term of one or two years; but only about 8.5 percent do so. On the other hand, the Christian missionary usually signs up for life. It is not uncommon for missionaries to remain on the field for thirty or forty years, health permitting. Others have rounded out half a century of service before calling it quits. By that time they are so immersed in the life and culture of the host country that only an ultimatum from headquarters will fetch them home. Given their way, they would prefer to die and have their bones buried in the land of their adoption. And how they are loved and revered by the national Christians! Consecration and continuity are a blessed bond.

Seventh, the Peace Corps is only ten years old and already it is showing signs of senility. It is doubtful if it will outlast the seventies. In contrast, the Christian mission is a venerable institution, old in years but young in spirit. It is part of the church universal, and as such it will never "like earth's proud empires pass away." It will continue to prosper and propagate until the knowledge of the glory of the Lord covers the earth as waters cover the sea (Hab 2:14).

8

THE NONPROFESSIONAL
MISSIONARY: GOOD OR BAD?

THE NUMBER OF AMERICANS living abroad has increased dramatically since World War II. Much of this is due to the military alliances we have with over forty other countries. In addition American business firms have greatly expanded their overseas operations. These overseas Americans may be divided into several categories: military personnel, government and diplomatic personnel, business and professional people, Peace Corps volunteers, and missionaries.

Thirty years ago almost all Americans in Africa were missionaries. Today they are outnumbered by persons in nonreligious occupations. This dramatic shift in the balance of American personnel overseas points up the vast potentialities of a nonprofessional missionary career.

Perhaps we should begin with a definition. A nonprofessional missionary is any dedicated Christian who lives and works overseas under nonreligious auspices, and who uses his secular calling as an opportunity to give his personal witness to Jesus Christ.

OBSERVATIONS

Some general observations are in order before we discuss the pros and cons of such an arrangement.

The lay apostolate is not new. In the first century there were no missionary societies such as we have today and there were few professional missionaries outside the apostolic group. The gospel was spread far and wide throughout the Roman Empire by laymen—soldiers, slaves, merchants, and even displaced persons.

117

Luke informs us that those that were scattered abroad upon the persecution that arose about Stephen went everywhere preaching the gospel (Ac 8:4). Some of them went into nearby Judea and Samaria (Ac 8:1); others went as far afield as Antioch and Cyprus (Acts 11:19). Speaking of the converts in the mission church at Thessalonica, Paul said, "From you sounded out the word of the Lord not only in Macedonia and Achaia, but also in every place your faith to God-ward is spread abroad" (1 Th 1:8).

Edward Gibbon, in his *Decline and Fall of the Roman Empire,* explains the rapid growth of Christianity in the early centuries by the fact that it became the sacred duty of every convert to speak of his newfound faith to his friends and neighbors. Will Durant in his book, *Caesar and Christ,* makes the same point. "Nearly every convert, with the ardor of a revolutionary, made himself an office of propaganda."[1]

With no weapon but truth and no banner but love these single-minded, warmhearted followers of Jesus traveled by land and sea to all parts of the empire. Wherever they went they gladly shared their faith with friends, neighbors, and strangers. As slaves, traders, and, later on, soldiers, they used their secular calling to advance the cause of Christ. Even as exiles they carried the contagion of their faith to distant shores and inhospitable regions.

Even in modern times, when missionary endeavor has been along organizational lines, we have not been entirely without nonprofessional missionaries. The first Protestant missionary to China, Robert Morrison, though a member of the London Missionary Society, was also for a time an official interpreter for the East India Company. William Carey supported himself and his colleagues by teaching at Fort William College in Calcutta. His salary of $6,000 a year helped to support the missionary enterprise at Serampore.

Other laymen, with no missionary society connections, have had a remarkable ministry in non-Christian countries. Outstanding among these was a military man, Captain Janes, who taught military science at Doshisha University in Japan. So dynamic was his witness that out of that university came the famous Kumamoto Band, composed mostly of samurai, which made such an impact on the emerging church in Japan.

1. Will Durant, *Story of Civilization,* vol. 3, *Caesar and Christ* (New York: Simon & Schuster, 1944), p. 602.

There is nothing wrong or undesirable about the lay apostolate.
Jesus Christ needs His witnesses in all walks of life. In the body
of Christ there are various offices and ministries. Not all are
apostles, prophets, or preachers. In fact these professional classes
represent a tiny minority of the whole church. The important
thing is not whether one is a professional minister or missionary,
but whether he is dedicated to the proposition that the gospel by
its very nature must be shared with all the world. Whether a
person becomes by profession a merchant or a missionary is for
God to decide. The merchant is not a second-class citizen in the
kingdom of Heaven. So far as holy orders are concerned, many
are called but few are chosen. Not every Christian is a missionary but every Christian is, or should be, a witness. To fail to
witness is a denial of one's faith.

*Nonprofessionals are a supplement to, not a substitute for, regular
missionary work.* An exception, of course, would be the countries
now closed to the professional missionary. Afghanistan is a classic
example. Officially this country is tightly closed against all Christian missionaries; but it is common knowledge that today there are
over one hundred dedicated Christians in Afghanistan, most of
them from the Christian countries of the West, who are serving
the government and people in the name and spirit of Jesus Christ.
But in other countries the nonprofessional missionary is not working in competition with the professional missionary. Where possible he will identify with the Christian church and channel his
converts into the church.

There should be no rivalry between the two kinds of missionary.
Both represent the same Lord; both serve the same cause; both
seek to extend the same kingdom. Where the professional missionary is present, the nonprofessional missionary fills a supporting role in church building. Where the professional missionary is
absent, the nonprofessional missionary will have to carry the full
load himself.

*Nonprofessionals should be aware of the limitations of their call-
ing.* Few of them have had any theological training. Fewer still
have any knowledge of the great non-Christian religions of the
world. These two facts will put the nonprofessional missionary at
a serious disadvantage when he comes to witness for Christ. One

must have a thorough understanding of his own faith before he can explain it to a person of another faith. It is one thing to share one's faith with his fellow Americans, whose cultural background is similar to his own. It is quite another thing to present the claims of Christ to a Hindu, a Buddhist, or a Muslim. To do this successfully one must have a clear understanding of his own faith and at least a working knowledge of these other non-Christian religions. Otherwise the non-Christian is likely to get the best of the dialogue. Not every Christian layman can articulate his own faith in terms that are meaningful to non-Christians.

Moreover, the company for which he works, whether private firm or government agency, may place certain restrictions on the religious activities of its employees. He may be forbidden to "talk religion" during working hours. Even in his leisure time he may be expected to socialize with his own expatriate group. Such restrictions are not unknown in American communities overseas.

The nonprofessional missionary, no less than the professional missionary, is affected by the political climate prevailing in the host country. The United States is at once the best loved and most hated nation in the world today. Time was when an American passport was the most desirable in the world. This is no longer so. The cold war, our voting record in the United Nations, our foreign aid program, our involvement in Indochina, and the tensions between the "have" nations and the "have not" nations, directly affect the status of Americans overseas. If a government decides to discriminate against Americans residing in its territory, no distinction is made between missionaries and nonmissionaries. When restrictions are imposed, *all* Americans are involved. It is a mistake to assume that the nonprofessional missionary will fare better than the professional missionary.

The nonprofessional missionary will need to be a strong character with firm convictions and much courage. The professional missionary has many built-in safeguards. He is a member of a team and has all the advantages of Christian fellowship and counsel. He lives and works in an atmosphere conducive to holiness. He has many Christian friends, missionary and national; and in times of discouragement they may prove to be a tower of strength. But the nonprofessional missionary may have to stand all by himself.

Certainly he lives and moves, for the most part, in a climate that is hostile to the Christian faith and inimical to spiritual growth. If he is to hold his own against the insidious influence of the world around him, he will have to be a person of sterling character and strong convictions. The pressure from his peer group to conform to the life-style of the non-Christian community of which he is a part will be enormous. Only with the utmost tenacity will he be able to maintain any kind of Christian witness. He will discover in no time at all that it is easier to drift with the current than to swim against it. More than one lay Christian has started out with high hopes and great expectations, only to fall by the way when the going got rough. Unable to "go it alone," he has ended up a moral and spiritual shipwreck.

The teaching profession offers the best opportunity for the non- ✗ *professional missionary.* The classroom situation has much to offer. To begin with, in the Orient and to a lesser degree in Africa, the teaching profession is held in high esteem. In Confucian culture the scholar occupies the highest station in society. Second, the teacher is the captain of his class and can do pretty much what he likes in his own classroom. Third, the dialogue of the classroom provides a natural setting for a discussion of the Christian faith. Fourth, the teacher is dealing with young people who are still in the process of intellectual maturation. Their minds are not yet set; consequently they are open to new ideas. They are not averse to change. Fifth, the students of today are the leaders of tomorrow. As such they represent the greatest potential of all groups on the mission field. Sixth, there is less frustration in the classroom than in any other situation in which the nonprofessional missionary may find himself. In other vocations he is likely to be all tied up in official red tape, bureaucratic control, political rivalry, vested interests, community squabbles, social and religious taboos, and a host of other problems; whereas in a school system he has an established institution, a structured program, a captive audience, and a forward-looking and ongoing community. Of course, he will make more money in business or government; but if it is an opportunity for effective Christian witness he is looking for, then the teaching profession is his best bet.

When the political situation explodes, the nonprofessional mis-

sionary is no better off than the professional missionary. The notion is growing that unless the Christian missionary is engaged
directly in nation building he is not really making much of a
contribution to the host country. Consequently he is the least desirable of all expatriates. From this it is deduced that when
trouble breaks out the first person to be expelled is the professional missionary. But the events of the past twenty-five years do
not bear this out.

According to *Time* magazine, in this postwar period almost one
hundred buildings owned by the United States government in
various parts of the world have been destroyed. And no one
knows how many times the American flag has been burned in anti-
American demonstrations. In contrast, very few mission buildings
—churches, schools, hospitals, or missionaries' residences—have
been destroyed. When embassy buildings have been attacked
and USIS libraries burned to the ground, church and mission
buildings in the immediate vicinity often have been spared. Apart
from Zaire, relatively few missionaries have lost their lives by
hostile action. In several countries the Peace Corps volunteers
have been asked to leave, while the missionaries have been permitted to remain. It would appear that the peoples and governments of the world have in this postcolonial period come to realize
that the missionaries are their best friends.

*Prospective nonprofessional missionaries would do well to search
their hearts to make sure that their motives are pure in God's
sight.* No one who understands the treachery of the human heart
will want to deny the fact that even the best of us are susceptible
to temptation. When we are emotionally involved in our own
decisions, it is easy to misinterpret the will of God. Man's capacity
for self-deception is absolutely enormous; and none of us is free
from this danger. It is just possible that a person may be called
by God to full-time missionary work; but for reasons of his own
he prefers to settle for the nonprofessional status.

This kind of temptation is extremely strong for several reasons.
It affords the person involved an opportunity to serve the Lord
outside the establishment, which is under attack these days. Also,
it makes it possible for him to be a missionary in fact without the
stigma of being a missionary in name. Moreover, it enables him to

function without the restrictions necessarily imposed by a mission board. With so many things going for it, the nonprofessional role is very attractive. Under such conditions it is easy for a dedicated person to assume that the more attractive role is God's will for him. It *may* be God's will. In that case he should be encouraged to pursue the matter with all the vigor at this command. Only let him be sure that he is not mistaking his own preferences and predilections for the will of God.

It is not an either/or proposition. Here is one instance when a person can have his cake and eat it too. It is possible nowadays to be a member of a mission, with all the rights and privileges pertaining thereto, and at the same time hold a teaching position in a secular college or university. Many missions not only permit but encourage their members to accept teaching positions in non-mission institutions. The Sudan Interior Mission has made a commitment to the government of Nigeria to supply a certain number of teachers for the public schools. The Africa Inland Mission has done the same in Kenya. Alas, neither mission has been able to fill the quota it assumed. These teachers are members of their respective missions; at the same time they are employees of the government and are paid with state funds. The Overseas Missionary Fellowship, operating in East Asia, has loaned a number of its workers to secular colleges and universities. One of them is preparing the curriculum for the study of Christianity to be used in all government schools throughout Indonesia. The North Africa Mission has similar plans for dedicated Christians wishing to work in secular capacities in North Africa. If they wish, they may be members of the North Africa Mission. Arrangements differ from mission to mission and from country to country. In some instances these teachers are full members of the mission; in others they are associate members. In either case, they have the best of both worlds.

ADVANTAGES

The nonprofessional may gain access into countries closed to the professional missionary. The Universal Declaration of Human Rights, prepared by the United Nations, has a very strong article on religious freedom, including freedom to change one's religion.

All but a handful of the 132 member nations have signed the declaration. But in spite of all the fine talk about religious freedom there are still countries where it exists only in theory. This is especially true of the Muslim countries of the Middle East and North Africa. It was not until the 1950s that the professional missionary was admitted to Nepal and Somalia. Only recently has he been allowed into Yemen. He is still unable to enter Afghanistan and Saudi Arabia.

But in all of these countries there are large numbers of expatriates serving in various capacities, either with their own governments or with the government of the host country. Others are engaged in business enterprises, and still others are in the professions. Countries such as Syria and Iraq, which broke off diplomatic relations with the United States during the Six Day War in 1967, are for the time being out of bounds to all American missionaries.

Others countries in the future may close their doors to the professional missionary. Such countries as India, Malaysia, Singapore, Surinam, and Thailand are tightening up on visa requirements; consequently the number of missionaries in those countries is gradually decreasing. In the light of this trend it is imperative that the Christian church seek other ways of getting the gospel to the ends of the earth. We must learn to be more flexible. If traditional methods fail, we should be prepared to adopt other modes of operation. There is nothing sacred about methods. Paul adopted one approach to the Jews and another to the Gentiles. He became all things to all men that by all means he might win men to Christ.

The nonprofessional missionary is a missionary and as such deserves the support of the Christian community in the homeland. He will not require any financial aid; but he will stand in constant need of moral and spiritual support; and this the church should be ready and willing to give. His name and picture should appear on the missionary roster in the foyer. If he is wise, he will keep the home church informed of his ministry and movements. He, no less than the professional missionary, stands in need of prayer support. He too wrestles not against flesh and blood, but against demonic forces which are part of the kingdom of Satan which Jesus Christ came to destroy.

The nonprofessional enjoys a measure of glamor and prestige. The image of the professional missionary has been tarnished at home and overseas. He is not the hero he was in the nineteenth century. Moreover, because he is engaged largely in religious work, the government of the host country does not consider that he is making a contribution to nation building. The nonprofessional missionary has no such handicap. In the eyes of the host country he is a secular person with a secular calling, and anything he does contributes directly or indirectly to nation building. In this sense he enjoys a greater measure of prestige than the professional missionary, who gives all his time to gospel preaching and church planting.

Moreover, the nonprofessional missionary is free from the stigma of "proselytizing." Coming from a so-called Christian country, he is assumed to be a Christian; but he is not expected to talk about religion, much less try to make converts to the Christian faith. Most Americans living abroad would call themselves Christians, but their religious convictions are not strong enough to prompt them to share their faith with non-Christians. Most of them prefer to travel incognito. Hence they pose no threat to the established religions of the host country. This being so, the nonprofessional missionary, so far as his status is concerned, enjoys the freedom of action that comes from neutrality. While he himself is a dedicated Christian, his official role is that of the businessman, the professor, or the diplomat. And when he talks about his religion, he does so in a casual, nonprofessional fashion. He has no axe to grind. He has no vested interests.

Financial remuneration is greater. Church workers and school teachers have always been among the lowest paid professional groups. In the past ten or fifteen years the plight of the teachers has been greatly relieved. Pastors are still at the bottom of the scale. Even so, they are better off than the missionaries, many of whom go right off the graph! One missionary kid, when applying for a scholarship, was called in by the college financial officer and questioned about the annual income reported by his parents. When the missionary kid insisted that the figure was correct, the officer replied, "It can't be correct! No one in the United States today can live on that kind of salary." Which only proves that the upper half of society doesn't know how the lower half lives.

It is a shame that the Christian church in the United States has permitted its full-time workers to live so long on the border line of poverty. In some parts of the country Christian organizations are still paying their employees less than the minimum wage established by law. Even so, the pastor is better off than the missionary. If the pastor's salary is not in hand at the end of the month, the church board will call an emergency meeting and make up the difference. But no one is there to go to bat for the missionary when his remittance falls below the norm, and the norm barely enables him to keep body and soul together. Almost every mission has missionaries on its roll for whom *full* support is not provided. The missionaries are expected "to live by faith," while the church members at home enjoy all the creature comforts of an affluent society. Some church members spend more on their summer (or winter) vacation than the missionaries get in a whole year.

In stark contrast to the missionaries are the business and professional people who are sent overseas by their companies. To induce them to live abroad their firms usually raise their salaries in addition to giving them a cost-of-living bonus that will provide them with all kinds of household servants to take the place of the timesaving mechanical gadgets they had at home. A special allowance is provided to take care of the education of the children. Fully paid furloughs come along every two or three years. And all these benefits are over and above the basic salary which, to begin with, may be three or four times what the missionary gets.

Thus the nonprofessional missionary, whether employed by an American firm or working for the host government, will be better off than the professional missionary. He will be able to provide himself and his family with the luxuries as well as the necessities of life. He will be able to pay all his bills and have something left over for travel, recreation, entertainment, and even investment. In these days when so many Americans are living "high on the hog" this is no mean advantage.

The nonprofessional has an opportunity to reach the elite. It is a well-known fact that most missionaries are working among the lower classes of society. Only a small number have access to the elite—and every country has its elite. Through the years the upper classes have been neglected, not so much by design as by necessity. There are several reasons for this. First, in a great many countries the elite represent a very small minority of 2 or 3 percent of the population. Second, in many non-Christian countries the stratification of society is so rigid that anyone working among the elite would automatically cut himself off from the rest of society. Third, the lower classes have the greatest needs and therefore get most attention. Fourth, the poor are much more open to the gospel and therefore represent a better investment of time and money. Fifth, the missionaries themselves have often felt inadequate to deal with the elite. Few missionaries come from wealthy families and therefore feel out of place among the rich. Others, with only a Bible school education, tend to shy away from the intellectuals. So for one reason or another the upper classes have been neglected.

The nonprofessional missionary, on the other hand, finds himself in an entirely different situation. He belongs to one of the professions; and other things being equal, he will work with fellow professionals in the host country. Engineers team up with engineers, or at least with budding engineers; lawyers with lawyers; diplomats with diplomats; bankers with bankers; surgeons with surgeons. Even in the Peace Corps an attempt is made to have the host government provide a counterpart to the American volunteer, even if he be only the community social worker.

If the nonprofessional missionary turns out to be a professor in a university, the principle still holds good. He will be working among fellow intellectuals, either students or teachers. Not only will he be accepted; he will be looked up to and respected. His academic and professional qualifications are usually impeccable. He is a specialist in his field, or he wouldn't be there in the first place. He has no difficulty in holding his own with the elite in any country. He is among peers, not patrons.

Consequently he doesn't have to force his way into the upper echelons of society; that's where he belongs. That's where he functions best. In such circles he will meet some perfectly charming people whose need for the gospel is just as great as that of the lower classes. Here, by the grace of God, he can bear his quiet witness for Jesus Christ; and his testimony will be all the more forceful for the fact that it comes spontaneously from the heart, prompted by deep personal convictions and supported by professional credentials of the highest order. In these high circles he will find inquiring minds, hungry hearts, and searching souls. And the persons thus won to Christ may be able, because of their position, to exercise an influence out of all proportion to their number.

DISADVANTAGES

I wish it were possible to say that the lay apostolate has only advantages and no disadvantages; but this is not so. Nothing in this life is *all* good. The good is always tempered with the bad. There are, alas, some disadvantages, and these should be discussed.

Lack of Christian fellowship. We who live in a Christian country and have membership in an active local church do not fully realize what we owe to Christian fellowship. We have had it so long and enjoyed it so much that we have come to take it for granted. The Sunday morning worship, the evening evangelistic service, the Sunday school for all ages, the midweek prayer and praise service, the home Bible classes, the committee meetings, the social gatherings, the choir rehearsals, the women's missionary society, the men's fellowship, the various youth groups, the married couples' club, the annual missionary conference, the vacation Bible school, and a host of other activities provide us with an endless source of inspiration, edification, and consolation—to say nothing of the many and varied religious programs brought right into our living rooms by way of radio and television. Surely the lines are fallen unto us in pleasant places. We have indeed a goodly heritage.

The situation on the mission field is quite different. The size of the Christian community varies greatly from 50 percent in some countries in Africa to less than 1 percent in many of the countries in Asia. For the most part the local churches are small and the fellowship is correspondingly weak. Quiet, orderly services, good "meaty" sermons, hearty Christian music are among the many things the professional missionary misses. I shall never forget my feeling of exultation when, after ten consecutive years in inland China, I attended my first English language worship service in Bowen Memorial (Methodist) Church in Bombay. The preacher was a handsome, brilliant Anglo-Indian who had received his theological education at Drew University. Such a well-prepared and thought-provoking sermon I had not heard in ten years. And what shall be said of the beautiful order of service, the content of the pastoral prayer, the choice selections by the well-trained choir, and the quiet and reverent atmosphere that prevailed throughout the entire service? All came cascading over my parched spirit like a sparkling waterfall on a hot and humid day. I shall always cherish the memory of that first service of my five-month stay in India.

If the professional missionary misses Christian fellowship, what shall be said of the plight of his nonprofessional counterpart? He is not a member of a mission so he cannot look in that direction for fellowship. The little church in town will not offer much help unless he understands the vernacular, and very few do. If he is located in the capital city, he will doubtless find a union church where the services are held in English. There he may or may not find the kind of fellowship he wants. Many of these union churches are liberal in their theological orientation and cater to a motley group of expatriates, many of whom are Christians in name only. The weekly program, if there is one, may have more in common with a social club than a Christian church.

Come Sunday the nonprofessional missionary may have nothing to do and no place to go. This will be particularly hard on him if he resides in a small town where there are no recreational or cultural activities. Complete lack of Christian fellowship over a long period of time may rob him of his joy and render him useless in the service of Christ.

Restrictions placed on expatriates by the host country. Religious freedom, like all other forms of freedom, can never be 100 percent. Communist governments regard all religions as the opiate of the people and place severe restrictions on religious activities. Muslim countries favor Islam and make the practice of other religions difficult if not impossible. Some countries, such as Nepal and Yemen, will allow foreign missionaries to operate in their territory but make it illegal for their own citizens to change their religion. Other countries, such as Burma and Syria, permit national churches to function but will not allow foreign missionaries to enter.

The nonprofessional missionary must not assume that because he is not a professional missionary he will be able freely to give his Christian witness in a given country. It stands to reason that countries which look askance on conventional missionary work are not likely to look with favor on the evangelistic efforts of the nonprofessional missionary. Peace Corps volunteers are warned by our government not to engage in religious activities overseas. They are free to attend church and to answer questions relating to their beliefs; but they are expected not to engage in any activities which might be construed as proselytizing.

In some instances the nonprofessional missionary is required to sign a statement agreeing not to engage in religious activities while overseas. Several such missionaries created a furor in Ethiopia when they held a Bible study class in their home in violation of their contracts. Only the timely intervention of Emperor Haile Selassie prevented their being expelled from the country. Muslim countries are especially sticky on this point. In most Muslim countries Islam is the state religion, and Muslims are off bounds to the Christian missionary, professional or nonprofessional. Pagan peoples and animistic tribes are fair game, but not Muslims. Conversion is a one-way street. A person may convert from Judaism or Christianity to Islam, but not from Islam to any other religion. It is true that in the Muslim countries of the Middle East religious minorities are tolerated and ancient Christian churches are permitted to exist; but only for the purpose of worship, not witness. An open attempt to convert a Muslim might easily lead to a communal riot.

In all countries where religious freedom is restricted the nonprofessional missionary will be at a serious disadvantage. He will need to be as wise as a serpent and as harmless as a dove. One false move and he may be asked to leave.

Limitations necessitated by time and strength. The first responsibility of the lay missionary is to his employer. He will be expected to give forty hours a week—sometimes more—to the work for which he is paid. The terms of his contract may not permit him to give an oral witness on the job, in which case his only opportunity to engage in Christian work will be after hours and on weekends. When the weekend rolls around, he may be so tired that he cannot face the extra effort required by Christian work. Either he or his wife may decide that the weekend is the only opportunity available for relaxation. We all know how difficult it is to get Christian laymen at home to give time to the church. People are too busy—or think they are—to attend the midweek prayer and Bible study. As for special week-night meetings, they have been eliminated in many churches for lack of support. If this is so on the home front, what reason is there to believe that the lay Christian on the mission field will act differently? He may start out with high resolve, but the limitations of time and strength may prove too much for him. It takes a very unusual Christian to stand up to the pressures of vocational life, the responsibilities of home and family life, and the demands of Christian service over a long period of time. Sooner or later lethargy sets in and he becomes weary in well doing. When this happens, the first thing to suffer is Christian service.

Language barriers make witness difficult. The average American remains overseas for two and a half years. During this time few ever bother to learn a foreign language; and even if they do, the time span is not long enough to ensure any degree of proficiency. Many expatriates carry on their professional work by means of interpreters provided either by the American firm or by the host government. These are available only for the eight hours each day when the person is on the job. They are not available for social contacts during the evening hours or the weekends. Without an interpreter the lay missionary is at a very serious disadvantage when it comes to witnessing for Christ. It is difficult enough to explain the Christian gospel to fellow Americans at home. How much more difficult it is to explain the gospel to non-Christian nationals of other countries! Of course many nationals, especially those in high positions, have a working knowledge of English and can be reached through that medium.

Limited contacts with the nationals. In most countries the expatriate tends to move in the narrow circles of the international community, where English is spoken. This is especially true of his free time. He may *work* with the nationals, but he *plays* with the Americans and other members of the international community. This unfortunate behavior on the part of Americans abroad has been graphically described in *The Ugly American,* in which the authors tell of the endless round of cocktail parties that go to make up the social life of the diplomatic corps in the large cities of Southeast Asia.[2]

In the heyday of colonialism the expatriates kept pretty much to themselves in their social contacts. They had their own swimming pools, golf courses, and tennis courts from which the nationals were excluded. Their social life was confined to these exclusive clubs. It was enough that they had to spend the working day in a strange environment. When evening came they retired to the sanctuary of the international community. There was almost no contact with the nationals outside office hours.

In recent years some progress has been made. Segregated clubs are no longer tolerated; but expatriates still tend to congregate with other expatriates. In some instances they live in a foreign enclave in the most affluent part of town and saunter forth only during the day. In a few countries the large oil companies provide housing for their American personnel on company property, making the isolation that much more complete. To keep in touch with life back home in the United States of America, they subscribe to the international editions of *Time* and *Newsweek.* For their day-by-day international news they listen to the "Voice of America." They live and move and have their being in a little patch of the United States set down in the heart of Caracas, Cairo, Kabul, or Khartoum. Their bodies are overseas, but their hearts and minds are back home in the good old USA.

The nonprofessional missionary often finds himself part of such an international community. He can, of course, break away from the American ghetto and establish social contacts with the people of the country; but it will require a strong personaltiy and a go-it-alone mentality on his part. The pressure to conform to the social patterns of his peer group will be enormous. He will require the wisdom of Solomon and the courage of Daniel to bridge the social gap between the two communities; and if he succeeds, he may incur the displeasure of the international community and the censure of the American firm for which he works.

If he cannot speak the local language, his contacts with the

2. Wm. J. Lederer and Eugene Burdick, *The Ugly American* (New York: Fawcett, 1963).

national churches will be minimal. Listening to a sermon in an unknown tongue is not particularly edifying. Curiosity may prompt him to attend one or two services, but after that he and his family will probably gravitate to the union church, where the service is in English and the worshipers are mostly expatriates. Under these conditions he will have little contact with the nationals, Christian or non-Christian.

Frustration is a perennial problem. It is common knowledge that frustration has dogged the steps of the professional missionary from the very beginning. What is not so well known is that the same thing is true of the business and professional man. This is particularly true of the wives of business and professional men, who have nothing to do, and all day to do it. Not a few businessmen have had to return to the States before their term of service was completed because their wives could not endure life in a foreign culture, where everything was so different from what they were accustomed to back home.

There are few persons more pathetic than the wives of American businessmen overseas. Without a knowledge of the language they have no way of communicating with the people. Shopping for the smallest item is an exercise in frustration. To make matters worse, they can't attend the movies or even watch television. With a staff of domestic servants to take care of the household chores they have all kinds of time on their hands, with nothing to do and no place to go. Little wonder that many of them spend their days playing cards and their evenings at cocktail parties.

Frustration is by no means confined to the wives; their husbands have their frustrations too! The American way of doing things may or may not appeal to the leaders in Africa, Asia, or even Latin America. They have their way of life and are in no great hurry to change. Promptness and efficiency, the hallmarks of American business, are not necessarily regarded as virtues in the Third World. Life there is lived at a leisurely pace. The business of making a living is not nearly so important as the art of living. As for improving life by newfangled gadgets and gimmicks, this has no great attraction for people who for centuries have been content with simple things. There are two ways in which a person can be rich. One is in the multiplicity of his possessions; the other is in the simplicity of his wants. Most persons in the Third World would cheerfully settle for the second. Consequently when American technicians try to introduce a better product or a more efficient method of production, the nationals are often indifferent. Such an attitude is the cause of deep frustration.

Even the Peace Corps has its problems with frustration. The people show little interest in new and better ways of doing things and so are loath to change. And if they do change under pressure from the volunteer, they frequently revert to the old way after the Peace Corps moves on. This is one reason why the casualty rate in the Peace Corps is 17.2 percent as compared with 2.5 percent for professional missionaries over the same period of time.

Is there a place for the nonprofessional missionary? Indeed there is. God needs His servants in all walks of life, at home and overseas. The Holy Spirit is sovereign. He chooses one person to be a professional missionary and another to be a nonprofessional. There should be no rivalry between them. Both are needed for the preaching of the gospel and the extension of the kingdom. Only let the nonprofessional missionary take cognizance of the pros and cons of the situation and be fully aware of the pitfalls peculiar to his calling.

9

THE SHORT-TERM MISSIONARY: PRO AND CON

ONE OF THE MOST DRAMATIC breakthroughs in modern missions is a new program known as Short Terms Abroad (STA). Some old-line denominations have had such a program for a long time. The United Presbyterians have made use of short-term missionaries for over half a century. Most of their short-termers were employed as teachers in their many educational institutions around the world. Until recently their numbers were never large. About 1960 the program was greatly expanded. By the mid 1960s two out of three missionaries were short-termers. In 1968 the denomination decided to make no more lifetime appointments. Since then two other denominations have done likewise—the Protestant Episcopal Church and the United Church.

The United Methodists began their short-term program in 1948. By the mid 1960s they had sent out over one thousand short-term missionaries. Another pioneer in this area was the Mennonite Central Committee (MCC). Its first group of twenty Paxmen went to Europe in 1951 to serve for two or three years in the refugee camps. Since then almost one thousand Paxmen have served in Asia, Africa, Latin America, and the Middle East. They work in such diverse fields as agriculture, mechanics, construction, maintenance, radio, education, relief goods distribution, and office work. Beginning in 1962 the MCC introduced a second program for teachers only, known as Teachers Abroad Program (TAP). Working almost exclusively in Africa, TAP in the past nine years has placed 250 teachers in strategic short-term positions.

One by one the other missions got in on the act. Today there is hardly a mission that does not have its own short-term program. The Protestant Episcopal Church has its Volunteers for Missions. The American Baptists have their Volunteer Services. The Southern Baptists have two short-term programs: the Missionary Associates Program launched in 1961, and the Missionary Journeymen Program begun four years later. The former makes it possible for men and women between thirty-five and fifty-nine years of age to serve a term overseas in projects that do not involve the learning of a foreign language. The second program is designed to enlist young people under twenty-seven years of age who want to use their talents to meet critical spiritual, educational, and physical needs overseas. Both programs offer one- or two-year terms of service. In 1969 the Southern Baptists sent out 258 new missionaries, of whom 100 were short-termers.

For some time the conservative evangelicals, represented by the Interdenominational Foreign Mission Association and the Evangelical Foreign Missions Association, tried to buck the tide. They held out as long as they could, but by 1960 they, too, were forced to come to terms with the short-term program. Why the sudden change? The answer is simple. They had no choice. They were not getting enough career missionaries to maintain their existing work, much less initiate new work. No mission prefers short-termers, but half a loaf is better than none. The universal law of supply and demand has been with us for a long time; and to date no one has been able to circumvent that law.

Thus it came about that the evangelical conservative boards began accepting short-term workers. One of the earliest to launch its program was the Sudan Interior Mission. In January, 1962, the mission sent out an appeal for twenty-five college graduates to proceed to Nigeria on a thirty-month program designed to provide qualified teachers for teacher training colleges. "Our need," the mission said, "is for many missionary teachers who had at least minimum qualifications. We underline 'missionary' because it is a prime qualification. We would be unable to use in our work individuals who were not first missionaries having mature Christian faith and a sound understanding of the Bible."

The Conservative Baptist Foreign Mission Society, the Christian and Missionary Alliance, and the Evangelical Free Church all launched their own short-term programs. Other mission boards followed in rapid succession. Today there are only a few of the nearly one hundred missions in the two associations that do not accept short-term missionaries.

The program takes various forms. The usual term is three years, though quite frequently the period of service is one or two years and sometimes as high as four years. Some missions have several programs from which the volunteer can choose—one-, two- or three-year programs.

Short-termers consist mostly of young people just out of college. Sometimes they take a year or two out of their college program and spend the time abroad. Most of them are single. Girls as well as fellows volunteer; indeed the girls usually outnumber the men, as they do among career missionaries. A second group of short-termers represent people at the other end of the age spectrum. These are retired persons who still have five or ten good years ahead of them and want to serve the Lord on the mission field. Indeed, some of them choose to retire early in order to lengthen their short-term missionary career. These people are known as second careerists, and their number is growing with every passing year. These older folks have several things going for them. At that advanced age married couples as well as single persons are free from family responsibilities. Most of them have a pension which renders them financially independent. Those who are sixty-five or older usually have Social Security benefits as well.

These people are usually able to pay their own way and take care of room and board on the field. In this as well as other respects, they represent a handsome gift to the missions under which they serve. Most of the single people in this category are teachers. On the mission field there are scores of schools for missionaries' children; most of them are hurting for lack of qualified teachers. With twenty-five or thirty years of teaching experience behind them, these second careerists are able to fill a vital role in the missionary ranks. Even without missionary experience, these older missionaries make wonderful hosts and hostesses in mission homes, or houseparents in schools for missionaries' children. Others with experience in bookkeeping, accounting, typing, and filing are able to fill vacant posts in mission offices, at home or

abroad, thus setting career missionaries free for more direct forms
of missionary service. There is no end to the helpfulness of these
second careerists.

Not a few older couples, as well as widows and widowers, visit
their children and grandchildren on the mission field, fall in love
with the people and the work, and decide to stay on for a year or
two to help out in various capacities.

Still other short-termers go abroad to perform a specific task;
when the task is completed they return home. A building con-
tractor spent a year in Bangladesh where he built a mission hospital. A Canadian doctor spends his annual vacation in a mission
hospital in Monrovia, Liberia.

POPULARITY OF THE SHORT-TERM PROGRAM

How are we to account for the sudden popularity of the short-
term program? Several factors readily come to mind.

Increasing mobility. Time was when a family living in Maine
would remain there for several generations. If a member of the
family ventured as far west as Boston, he was regarded as a world
traveler. Today the members of the younger generation are leaving Maine and not stopping until they get to California. If they
don't like the smog there, they can always move to Florida. If
they don't like the hurricanes there, they can migrate to Colorado.
By the time the second generation arrives on the scene, the family
may be scattered over half a dozen states of the Union. It is estimated that one of every four families moves every year.

Nor is it simply a matter of geography. People are forever
changing jobs. Young executives on the way up may work for
three or four firms before finding their niche. Few of them are
willing to make a long-term commitment to any one firm, even
General Motors. If Ford or Chrysler comes along with a better
offer, away they go.

Changing attitudes. Young people want to look before they leap.
They want to canvass all the options before making up their
minds. They want to get acquainted with the field and the work,
as well as the mission, before making their final decision regarding their life work. For this they have often been criticized. But
are they very different from the pastors here at home?

Very few pastors are extended a call sight unseen. In fact such a practice is almost unknown in this country. What is the procedure? A church without a pastor gets in touch with a preacher seeking a change. Arrangements are then made for the preacher to candidate in the church. The candidate and his family will spend a Sunday in the church, during which time he and the church will have an opportunity to find out as much as possible about each other. Only when the candidate is persuaded that the call comes from the Lord as well as from the church will he accept.

If this is the universal practice in the homeland, why should the procedure for service on the mission field be different?

Improved transportation. Hudson Taylor took five months from Liverpool to Shanghai in 1853. Today it is possible to reach any city in the world in a day or two. Jet travel, almost at the speed of sound, has made short-term missions not only a possibility but a live option.

Unsettled conditions. Since World War II there have been well over fifty wars of one kind or another, and literally hundreds of coups and countercoups. Whole continents, such as South America, are seething with unrest. In Africa some forty countries have achieved independence since 1960; one could number on the fingers of one hand the countries that have not experienced at least one coup, successful or abortive.

All this is in stark contrast to the situation that prevailed in Africa under the colonial system. For all its evils, colonialism did impose peace on the entire continent. Once the colonial system was established there were very few missionary martyrs. In fact, there were more martyrs in Zaire (Congo) from 1960 to 1964 than in the whole of Africa up to that time. This being so, it is hardly surprising that our young people are reluctant to commit themselves to Africa or Latin America for life.

Example of the Peace Corps. On the whole, the Peace Corps has been fairly successful; it has been well received in all but a few of the sixty countries in which it has worked. If the Peace Corps volunteer can do a good job in twenty-one months overseas, why can't the short-term missionary do the same?

Advantages of the Short-term Program

Appeals to today's youth. For the most part, young people are freedom-loving and easygoing, and do not want to be tied down to any one plan or program for any length of time. Moreover, it offers an opportunity to engage in missionary work without the "stigma" of being a missionary. They can return home after one term without being counted among the casualties. Also, it satisfies a legitimate desire to see the world and to enrich one's life and experience by serving the Lord in a completely different social and cultural milieu.

Helps solve manpower shortage. In some places this problem is so acute that career missionaries have had to postpone retirement or furlough because there was no one to take their place. In some instances it has been necessary to close a hospital during furlough for lack of qualified personnel. Evangelism and church planting are different. If the program stops when the missionary comes home on furlough, no great loss is incurred. The work can be resumed when the missionary returns. Institutional work, by its very nature, has to go on; and personnel must be found to fill positions that fall vacant.

Leads to a lifetime of service. In some of the historic denominations, more than 50 percent of their present career missionaries began as short-termers. Three denominations no longer accept career missionaries to begin with. All new missionaries are expected to serve for one or two short terms before making up their minds to become career missionaries.

The short-term program is still comparatively young, and reliable statistics are difficult to obtain. To further complicate the matter, the situation differs from mission to mission; but it is generally believed that 20 percent of the short-termers become career missionaries after one term abroad. Of those who spend two or more short terms abroad, 50 percent sign up for life, which means that in the long run the short-term program is a good thing for the cause of missions.

Of course there is no guarantee that the volunteers will be favorably impressed with what they find overseas. Most of them are "turned on" and come back with glowing reports. Others are "turned off" and do great harm on their return to this country. But even the ones who are "turned off" are by no means a total loss to the cause. If they could not adjust to missionary life and work during a short term, they would almost certainly have become casualties if they had signed up for life. If missionary work is not their "cup of tea," they might as well find this out early as late. Mistakes are made. To err is human. Divine guidance is never 100 percent certain—not after it has filtered through the human mind.

Every person is emotionally involved in his own understanding of the Lord's will for his life. Consequently it is impossible for him to be completely objective in his appraisal of a given situation involving his own interests, ambitions, and desires. The author is personally acquainted with several wonderful students who in their college days were enthusiastically dedicated to missionary work and were leaders in the Foreign Missions Fellowship; but they were disillusioned by a visit to the mission field. One of these is now a waitress in a Howard Johnson's restaurant. Another married a truck driver. Missionary work is not for everyone. We can only assume that those who are "turned off" by a visit to the mission field were never called to missionary work in the first place. It is good, both for the candidate and for the mission, that this fact be discovered as early as possible to avoid loss of time, money, and face.

Frees career missionaries for other duties. We hear a good deal these days about specialization; but the truth is that most missionaries, including specialists, are required to do double and triple duty, not because it is mission policy but simply of necessity. There are too few missionaries and too many jobs to fill. For instance, the medical missionary will be physician, surgeon, and administrator all in one. When the electrical equipment breaks down, he repairs it. When an epidemic of cholera breaks out, he becomes a public health officer in the community. The teaching missionary cannot confine his teaching to the Old Testament or the New Testament. There are not enough teachers for that kind of specialization. Sometime or other he will be required to teach nearly every subject in the catalog. In addition, he may be asked to act as dean of men or registrar. When the business manager goes on furlough, he may be asked to do the bookkeeping on the side.

In all such situations the short-termer is a veritable godsend. He can fill the gap and relieve the career missionary of the extra chores for which he has neither the time nor the training.

Brings blessing to stateside churches and colleges. The vast majority of short-termers return with glowing accounts of their time abroad. Almost to a man they affirm that the experience was an eye-opener. Even if they don't get back to the field, they will never be the same again. They are now sold on missions and will help sell missions to others. In this capacity they can do more for missions than career missionaries on furlough. Indeed, college students are more impressed with the reports of their fellow students than by anything the missionary might say. After all, most missionaries are over thirty! Besides, they have a vested interest in their own vocation; whereas the returning short-termer is believed to be more objective if not more impartial. Many Christian colleges have noticed an increased interest in missions since they launched their summer missionary programs.

Provides enthusiasm and idealism. Short-termers are almost all under twenty-five years of age, with all the freshness, initiative, and idealism of youth. They have none of the hangups that blur the vision and impede the progress of the veteran missionaries. One of their strengths is the mobility and adaptability that usually go with a person whose stay is temporary. Being young, they are more apt to be footloose and fancy-free. Being single, they can afford to run greater risks. Certainly they are able to identify with the youth of the host countries, adapt to their customs, and respond to their needs in a way that some of the older missionaries have not been able to do. Their free and easy manner, the informality of their dress, their practice of sitting on the floor, their desire to just "rap," their experiments in communal living, all enable the short-termer to get close to the people. After all, that's what missionary work is all about.

Problems Related to the Short-term Program

Like every other program, STA has its problems, some of which are rather serious.

Inexperience. Experience is a valuable asset in any endeavor; it is doubly valuable in a cross-cultural situation. Of course, the career missionary has the same problem at first, but by the time he returns for his second term, his mistakes are mostly behind him. He is now ready to make a real contribution to the spread of the gospel and the building up of the church. But the short-termer comes home just when he is beginning to function like a seasoned missionary. This is hard on everyone concerned, particularly the national Christians and leaders, who patiently endure the bluff and blunder of the young missionary in the hope that he will learn by his mistakes and be more of a blessing and less of a burden during his second term. But if there is no second term, they are doomed to another round of bluff and blunder. After breaking in nine or ten of these short-termers, they become weary in well doing.

Acculturation. It is of the utmost importance that missionaries understand and appreciate both the people and the culture of the land in which they serve. This takes time. It cannot be learned in thirteen easy lessons. It is naïve in the extreme to imagine that a three-hour course in general psychology will enable a person to understand the Oriental mind, or that a study in American sociology will enable one to understand and appreciate the various cultures found in the Third World. It usually takes a year or two to really feel at home in a culture other than one's own. The body can be transported to another part of the world in a matter of hours. It may take years for the soul to catch up. This is especially hard on the short-term worker who is just beginning to make his way and feel at home when his term is up.

Communication. Most missionary work involves some form of cross-cultural communication. To do effective work, the short-term volunteer should be able to speak the vernacular accurately and fluently. It is difficult to acquire fluency through a crash program of five or six weeks. Indeed, veteran missionaries constantly find themselves making blunders, especially in tonal languages. The right word expressed in the wrong tone will not only create misunderstanding, but in some cases will result in downright embarrassment to both speaker and hearer.

Short-termers who speak only English should be sent to English-speaking countries. They will get along fairly well in ex-British colonies where English is still the *lingua franca* if not the official language. One great advantage attaching to the short-term program launched from the United States or the Commonwealth countries is the fact that English is the most widely understood language in the world. It comes closer than any other language to being the world's *lingua franca*. When the Dalai Lama fled as as refugee from Tibet to India and was greeted by Prime Minister Nehru, the two conversed in English! Most of the speeches in the United Nations are made in the English language.

Persons going to Francophone Africa should be able to speak French. Those going to Latin America will find Spanish spoken in all countries except Brazil. Language is not usually a great problem for medical missionaries. The nature of their work does not require them to do much talking. If the medical tests reveal appendicitis, the surgeon goes to work and removes the offending member with little or no conversation. Also, in many countries nationals who study medicine are required to learn the medical terms in English. Fluency is a must for all teaching and preaching missionaries.

Interpretation, of course, is always a possibility, but it has its drawbacks. Can an interpreter be found? If so, is he fluent enough to pick up idiomatic expressions and translate them accurately? Then there is the time factor. To use an interpreter cuts the speaker's time in half. One or two lectures can be translated without much difficulty, but what about a series of thirty or forty lectures in a Bible school? It can be and has been done; but it requires much patience on the part of the speaker and just as much perseverance on the part of the listeners.

Expense. Regular air fare from Chicago to Johannesburg is $1,186 round trip; to New Delhi and back it is $1,478. If this amount is amortized over thirty-six months, it works out at $41 per month; but if the worker stays only one year, it averages out at $123 per month—just for transportation. Fourteen hundred dollars may not sound like a lot of money to affluent Americans; but it represents a mammoth sum to the Christians in India, where the per capita income is less than one hundred dollars a year. Whatever else may be said for the short-term program, it isn't cheap.

Generation-gap. The average age of the short-termer is about twenty-six years; that of the long-termer is much higher. This alone can create problems. Added to this is the fact that the career missionary is wiser, more mature, more experienced, and more patient than his younger counterpart. The newcomer, in his youthful enthusiasm, may criticize his senior colleague for his failure to initiate change, improve methods, correct mistakes, and hand over responsibility to others. The career missionary on his part may secretly resent the idealism, enthusiasm, and passion for action and reform that characterize today's younger generation. He has been around long enough to know that it is easier to see than to solve the major problems of the mission field. The older missionary may feel that his very seniority invests him with a certain degree of authority and prestige; while the short-termer may consider himself to be a second-class citizen. Under such conditions it is quite possible that a kind of "pecking order" may develop between the two groups.

Lack of continuity. Change is good; but it is possible to get too much of a good thing. We want change by all means; we also need stability, and stability cannot be achieved without a high degree of continuity. When we extol the virtues of the short-term program, we are generally thinking in terms of the mission and its recruiting problems. Seldom do we consider the needs and wishes of the national Christians and the church leaders on the mission field. To get some idea of their perspective, one need only imagine a church in the United States that undergoes a change of pastor every year or two. No church would voluntarily vote for that kind of arrangement. In rare circumstances it happens, but always without the approval of the church concerned. If the pastor is any good at all, the people will want him to stay for five or six years at least. If the church has more than two hundred families, it will take the new minister a year or two to really get to know his people—their names, their needs, and their notions.

It goes without saying that Christian work, abroad as well as at home, suffers from frequent interruption. What is needed on the mission field is more, not less, continuity. Indeed, with career missionaries coming home on furlough every four years, the problem of continuity is already acute. A problem that mission executives have always had to grapple with is how to provide substitutes for missionaries on furlough. Not infrequently positions have been left vacant, and the work has suffered accordingly. On occasion it has been necessary to take a general missionary out of his work to fill the personnel needs of a school or hospital when a missionary goes on furlough. With more and more short-term workers joining the missionary ranks, the. problem of continuity is greater than ever.

National church leaders have never been happy with the concept of furlough. Many of them have considered it unnecessary, certainly undesirable. Time and again they have asked the question: "Why do missionaries and their families have to go home to the United States every four or five years? They seem to be quite well in body and mind. Why the prolonged vacation? And if they must have a rest, could they not get it here in our country?" To add to their troubles they are never sure that, if and when the missionary returns, he will be reassigned to the same position. If they have these feelings with regard to career missionaries, what must be their attitude to the short-term missionary? They *know* he will not be back; nor will the one after him, nor the next one after him. No, the national church leaders do not take kindly to all the comings and goings of the missionaries, short- or long-term.

Imbalance. Even the most ardent supporters of STA do not suggest that the short-termer is a substitute for the career missionary. If the career missionary needs the short-termer, certainly the short-termer needs the career missionary. Indeed, he could hardly function without him. With the sudden and expanding popularity of the short-term program, there is a real danger that certain missions will find themselves with a serious imbalance in their roster. To work effectively the short-termer needs the counsel and guidance of the veteran missionary. A given mission can profitably absorb only a certain number of short-termers. If they become too numerous, the whole program is likely to get out of kilter.

In the early stages of the short-term program, the mission stands to gain; but after five or ten years the homebound traffic gets pretty heavy. Then the home office has to send out an ever-increasing number of new workers to keep the roster at full strength. More and more time must be spent filling the many vacancies created by returning short-termers. After a while the problem begins to snowball, and the mission, instead of needing a hundred new workers each year, needs two hundred.

Conditions of Success

The short-term program is no panacea. There is no guarantee that it will work. Certain conditions must be met if the program is to succeed.

Great care should be exercised in the choice of the short-termer. One must not assume that casualties do not occur in a short period of time. (The Peace Corps term of service is only twenty-one months, yet its casualty rate is 17.2 percent.) The candidate should be required to pass most, if not all, the tests demanded of the career missionary. It is for the volunteer's own good if he is kept home because of deficiencies. He should also be required to attend candidate school and benefit by the orientation given to the other missionaries. Moreover, as a short-termer he is susceptible to motives not usually present in the career missionary. Is he going along just for the ride, or to see the world, or to be exposed to an exotic culture, or even to enrich his own life? As fringe benefits these all have a legitimate place in his thinking; but they should never be the prime factor in his motivation.

Equal care should be shown in the choice of the field. A young person who would undoubtedly make the grade in Japan might easily fall flat on his face in Jordan. The person's health, education, interests, and skills should all be taken into consideration when assigning him to a specific country. If there is reason to believe that he will not feel at home in a primitive society, he should not be assigned to New Guinea. On the other hand, if he is a medical doctor, he should not be sent to Japan, where medical missions are practically nonexistent. If he is a died-in-the-wool capitalist and equates the free enterprise system with the kingdom of God, he may not be happy in India, Sweden, or Cuba.

The short-term worker should be assigned to a country where communication is not a problem. If he cannot speak the language with a fair degree of fluency he will most certainly be frustrated. If he knows Spanish, he ought to go to Latin America. If he can speak French, he will feel most at home in Francophone Africa. If he is familiar only with English, he can be sent to Anglophone Africa or any large city where English is understood by the people.

The particular skills of the short-termer should be matched with the existing needs on the field. The career missionary can afford to spend two or three years in search of a niche that he can fill with satisfaction to himself and profit to the church and mission; but not so the short-term worker. He has no time to look around or to find a job. The job should be waiting for the volunteer. For this reason it is advisable to place the volunteer in a highly structured program, usually in an institution, where he will know exactly what to do, can go to work immediately, and will have the satisfaction of making a worthwhile contribution. It is no accident that teaching has claimed the largest number of short-termers. They can arrive one day and start teaching the next. This is why it is important that the short-termer have a particular skill. He does not usually make an effective general missionary.

SUMMER MISSIONARY PROGRAM

A rapidly developing phase of STA is the Summer Missionary Program (SMP) adopted now by practically every mission board in the country. Not all American students who go to Europe each summer bask in the sun and sleep in the parks. An increasing number of them engage in missionary work.

One of the oldest and largest programs is Operation Mobilization (OM), sponsored by Send the Light, Inc. The first ventures took place in 1958, when George Verwer and twenty-one Moody students spent the vacation time distributing gospel literature in Mexico. From Mexico OM moved into Europe and today sends summer missionaries all over the world. During the summer of 1971 over a thousand young people engaged in literature distribution in Europe.

Cooperating with the mission boards are the various Bible schools and Christian colleges. The Foreign Missions Fellowship usually sponsors the program on the local campus, providing moral and financial support for the volunteers. Some of the larger colleges send as many as forty or fifty students overseas each summer. The program lasts about ten weeks, allowing the students plenty of time to get back for the opening of school in September. Upon their return the students share their experiences with their fellow students. On some campuses the entire spiritual climate has been changed as a result of this kind of SMP.

A fairly high percentage of the SMP students later sign up for the short-term program, and go on to become career missionaries. In recent years SMP has become exceedingly popular, with thousands of young people joining it. A recent questionnaire was filled in by sixty-five of the ninety-five missions in the EFMA/IFMA groups. In 1966 they reported a total of 308 who participated in the SMP. By 1969 the figure had jumped to 974. In 1970 the figure almost doubled to 1,784.

There is no doubt that there is a burgeoning interest on the part of our young people in all forms of short-term missionary work; so much that at least two organizations have been formed for the sole purpose of promoting short terms abroad. They are Christian Service Corps, 1501 Eleventh Street N.W., Washington, D.C. 20001; and Short Terms Abroad, P.O. Box 575, Downers Grove, Illinois 60515. The latter publishes an annual directory listing openings for short-term missionaries. The *1973 Directory* lists 5,600 specific openings reported by 179 mission agencies in all parts of the world.

10

CLOSING DOORS: FACT AND FICTION

IN THE POSTWAR PERIOD we have heard a great deal about closing doors. Missionaries on furlough have reminded us ad nauseum that in their part of the world they have "five more years" or "ten more years," as the case may be. Dozens of books have been published with such provocative titles as *Missions in Crisis; Missions in Revolution; Missionary, Go Home.* And only the Lord knows how many magazine articles of this kind have appeared in the last twenty-five years. We seem to have a pathological preoccupation with *closing* doors. Nobody talks about *opening* doors. In fact, we have talked so long about closing doors that we have come to believe our own story. Consequently many Christians are about to write off the missionary movement because it has no future.

One reason for the prevailing pessimism is the failure of the mass media to give us the full picture. Newspapermen are interested in news; and news, by definition, must be exciting if not sensational. "Business as usual" holds no appeal for the mass media. When several hundred missionaries evacuated Zaire in the summer of 1960, the secular press published pictures and articles of the event. When those same missionaries returned to Zaire only six months later, none of the press services picked up the story. The average American read about the exodus. He heard nothing about the return. Naturally, he came to only one conclusion—Zaire is closed.

Is it possible to separate the fact from the fiction? After all, there are almost 50,000 Protestant missionaries in over one hundred countries of the world, in any one of which the political situation may change overnight. To keep abreast of the international news, one needs a hotline to the United Nations Information Bureau. Nevertheless, in spite of the difficulties, it is possible to acquire a reasonably accurate picture of the world scene vis-à-vis Christian missions. The following observations will help to place the problem in proper perspective.

1. Actually, very few doors have closed in the last twenty-five years. In the whole of East Asia only six countries have expelled the missionaries: China, Mongolia, North Korea, North Vietnam, Cambodia, and Burma. The first four countries closed when the Communists came to power; and it must be admitted that the mass evacuation of mainland China in the early 1950s was the greatest reverse ever suffered by the modern missionary movement.

In the vast continent of Africa some forty nations have received their independence since 1960. Only one—Republic of Guinea—has expelled the missionaries, and even there the expulsion has not been complete. A skeleton force remains.

In the Muslim world the picture is somewhat more somber, owing mostly to the fact that the United States has given moral and material support to Israel, thus antagonizing the Arab states. During the Suez crisis in 1956, and again during the Six Day War in 1967, missionaries were evacuated in large numbers from various parts of the Middle East. Several Arab countries broke off diplomatic relations with the United States and to date have not restored them. When the dust settled some of the missionaries were able to return; others were not. American missionaries particularly find themselves in the crossfire of the Arab-Israeli conflict; British and European missionaries have fared better. At the present time four countries, Libya, Iraq, Saudi Arabia, and Syria, are closed. Turning to Latin America, we find that not a single country is closed to Christian missionaries. Guyana is tightening up on new missionaries entering the country, but other missionaries are still there. Even in Cuba a handful of missionaries are carrying on.

If we add them all up, we discover that fewer than a dozen countries have expelled the missionaries in this postwar period.

2. Other doors might close in the near future. It is conceivable that India, with a population of over half a billion, might close its doors to the Western missionary. Visas are increasingly difficult

to obtain; consequently the number of missionaries is slowly diminishing. Of the applications for missionary visas processed through the National Christian Council of India, 81 percent were granted in 1966, only 56 percent in 1968. Even so, there are still some 5,000 Christian missionaries in India. At present the granting or withholding of visas is quite haphazard. It would be premature to regard the exclusion of all foreign missionaries as a foregone conclusion. It is true, however, that the prestige of the missionary has been dropping, and his status today is rather precarious. The chief complaint is that of proselytizing. The fact that there are political as well as religious implications to this charge makes it rather serious. Several of the state governments have introduced legislation designed to curb, if not stop, all missionary activity. In 1967 several missionary families, American, Canadian, and Dutch, were expelled from Assam on charges that they "helped rebel uprisings." Some eight other missionaries were informed that their residence permits would not be renewed when they expired. The central government has tried to steer a middle course between the anti-missionary sentiment of the Hindu militants and the freedom of religion guaranteed by the constitution; but it can go only so far in defending missionaries in "sensitive areas." The United States' opposition to India's "invasion" of East Pakistan (Bangladesh) in December 1971 did nothing to ingratiate American missionaries with either the Indian government or the Indian people.

Malaysia has restricted missionary residence to ten years; after that he may not return, though exceptions have been made. Thailand has limited the number of foreign residents by establishing an annual quota. Missionaries without permanent visas must leave to renew their visas every ten weeks. Within the past year Singapore, the mecca of Christian missions in Southeast Asia, has made visas more difficult to obtain. Since the sudden and dramatic change in American policy towards Communist China, the government on Taiwan might well clamp down on new missionaries wishing to enter the country.

Two countries in Africa—Angola and Mozambique—have a rapidly dwindling missionary population. For almost a decade the Portuguese colonial administration permitted missionaries to leave but not return. Two missions decided to pull out altogether rather than submit to restrictions which they considered unacceptable. One mission, the Southern Baptist, managed to reverse the flow of traffic. Its first missionaries entered Angola in 1968.

The situation in Morocco is cause for some concern. A very successful Bible correspondence course, advertised in the newspapers and handled through the postal system, brought requests from 40,000 Muslims, representing every town in the country. As a result, the government cracked down on the Gospel Missionary Union, which sponsored the Bible correspondence course. By 1973 only three of its workers were in Morocco. The missionaries belonging to other missions, however, are still there. Naturally they are apprehensive for their own future; but they carry on courageously on a day-to-day basis, content to leave their fate in the hands of a sovereign God.

In January 1970 several Methodist missionaries were given twenty-four hours to leave Algeria. The government accused them of engaging in "subversive activities." The other missionaries in Algeria were allowed to remain. In recent years Nigeria, the largest country in Africa, has adopted a hard line against American missionaries entering the country; but Commonwealth missionaries are admitted more freely.

In South America only one government, Guyana, is not allowing new or returning missionaries into the country. The Communist party, very strong in Guyana, is doubtless behind this move. It remains to be seen what policy Chile, now under a Marxist regime, will adopt toward American missionaries. To date the evangelicals there have enjoyed an unprecedented measure of freedom. If President Allende, however, is a genuine Communist and remains in power for any length of time, there is sure to be a gradual erosion of freedom, in which case American missionaries are likely to become *persona non grata*.[1] Most missionaries left Cuba about the time Fidel Castro came to power in January 1959, but this they did on their own; Castro did not expel them. Some missionaries, mostly non-Americans stayed on; others have been permitted to return for short periods.

3. Some countries are assumed to be closed, but in fact they are still open, at least partially. Sudan is a classic example. In 1964 some three hundred missionaries, most of them Roman Catholic, were expelled from the three southern provinces. Immediately

1. A military coup ousted the communist regime in September 1973.

people began talking about Sudan as a closed land. This is not true. There are still missionaries in several places in the north, including the capital city of Khartoum. After the Simba uprising in the fall of 1964 and the murder of Dr. Paul Carlson and others, it was taken for granted that the Christian mission in Zaire was finished. Here again, we assumed too much. There have been three separate evacuations in Zaire; but never at any time was more than 50 percent of the missionary force involved. Cuba and India are sometimes referred to as closed countries; but, as we have seen, this is incorrect.

4. Some doors that we feared would close are still open. The largest of these is India. During World War II when Mahatma Gandhi was carrying on his "Quit India" campaign against the British, the missionaries there feared that if India ever got its independence they would have to leave along with the British Raj. This has not happened. During the Mau Mau Rebellion, led by Jomo Kenyatta in the 1950s, the situation in Kenya was extremely grave. When Kenyatta came to power in 1963, the missionaries had their bags packed, ready for sudden evacuation. But Kenya has turned out to be one of the more stable countries in Africa, and President Kenyatta has more than once paid public tribute to the work of the missionaries. In 1965 it looked as if Indonesia would be taken over by the Communists; but the Communist-inspired coup of October 1 proved abortive. The missionaries are still there in full force and revival has swept an estimated two million persons into the kingdom of God. Too often we have been unnecessarily fearful of the many storm clouds on the political horizon, forgetting that our God "rides upon the storm."

5. Closed doors do not necessarily remain closed forever; they have a way of opening again. For ten years—from 1948 to 1958—Colombia was closed to all new and returning missionaries. During that time there was a civil war which claimed the lives of 300,000 persons. The Roman Catholic Church, taking advantage of the unsettled conditions, carried out a widespread persecution of the evangelicals. Churches were destroyed, pastors were killed, and schools were closed. But in 1957 Dictator Rojas Pinilla was toppled from power, and a new, more liberal regime was installed. Immediately the tide changed and missionaries were once again

permitted to enter the country. Today there are more missionaries in Colombia than at any time in the past one hundred years; and they have opportunities undreamed of ten short years ago. During World War II Ethiopia, Korea, and Japan were all closed to Christian missionaries; but since the return of peace these countries are again the scene of intense missionary activity. Indeed, there are many more missions in Japan and Korea now than there were prior to the war. When Cambodia broke off diplomatic relations with the United States in 1965, all missionaries were expelled from the country. Five years later they were back in full force. Even the Communist countries of Eastern Europe show signs of loosening up. Bibles are being imported into some countries and printed in others. Billy Graham and other evangelists from the West have held meetings in most of them.

6. In the last twenty years some doors have opened for the first time. Strange that we are so quick to learn of closing doors, but seldom hear of opening doors! For hundreds of years the Hindu kingdom of Nepal was sealed off from all contact with the rest of the world. Then in 1954 the door opened, and the United Mission to Nepal (UMN), comprising at that time some thirty missionaries belonging to ten different boards, entered the country. The mission signed a five-year contract with the government agreeing to confine its activities to educational, medical, agricultural, and technical work. There was to be no religious work. The UMN is still there, only now it comprises twenty-nine boards and 130 missionaries. It has work in a dozen towns and villages, and a small group of Christians is to be found in twenty centers. Besides the UMN, other missions are now there: the Nepal Evangelistic Band, Wycliffe Bible Translators, International Christian Fellowship, and others.

Equally intriguing, though less fruitful, has been the work begun in Somalia. Here the dominant religion is Islam. It opened its doors to Protestant missionaries in the early 1950s. The first mission to enter, in 1953, was the Eastern Mennonite Board of Missions and Charities, followed a year later by the Sudan Interior Mission. Here again proselytizing is a criminal offense, and the two missions must exercise great care in the way they go about their missionary work. Evangelism and church planting are frowned upon; but in spite of the many restrictions the two missions have been able to make considerable headway. Though it is not possible to organize churches, there are small groups of believers in nine centers. A bookstore in the capital is doing a thriving business. In 1966 the SIM announced the translation of the complete New Testament into the Somali language. All missionary work was terminated by government action in 1973.

Other countries, which for hundreds of years have been closed to the Christian missionary, are now showing signs of opening up. Yemen, the most backward country in the world, is the latest country to open its doors to the Christian missionary. The year was 1964. The mission was the Southern Baptist. The pioneer missionary, Dr. James Young, entered Yemen at the invitation of the Minister of Health. Since that time the Southern Baptists have established clinics and hospitals in various parts of the country.

For years the Red Sea Mission Team tried to enter Yemen, but not until 1970 was permission finally granted them. When it was, it was with the full knowledge that the Christian Scriptures would be distributed throughout the country. In fact Dr. Gurney presented the immigration officer with a red clothbound copy of the New Testament. After reading it, he asked for six additional copies to be given to his subordinates. Today the RSMT has medical missionaries in several cities.

Afghanistan is officially closed to all missionaries; but at present there are a hundred dedicated Christians in the country for the sole purpose of serving the government and the people in the name and spirit of Jesus Christ. Three Christian congregations of expatriates have been organized, and one Christian church had been erected.[2] These are off bounds to Afghan nationals except for Christmas, Easter, and funeral services. A major breakthrough occurred in November 1969, when a Youth for Christ Teen Team visited Kabul and presented a sacred concert. Over seven hundred people of the international community and of the nation's intelligentsia crowded into the ballroom of the Intercontinental Hotel to hear "Music with a Message." The following day they were featured on the front page of the *Kabul Times*. The president of Radio Afghanistan called the musical group a "holy delegation." A cabinet minister referred to their visit as "a light from God." All this in a staunch Muslim country which is officially closed to Christian missionaries!

2. The church building was demolished by government action in 1973.

7. Closed doors are not necessarily unmitigated tragedies. Missionaries, like anybody else, are inclined to have an inflated opinion of their own importance. Now and again it is well to remind ourselves that *if need be* God can get along without us. Any sovereign state has the right to expel undesirable aliens. But it is one thing to get rid of the missionaries; it is another to get rid of Almighty God. Heaven is His throne and earth is His footstool. It is impossible to banish Him from any part of His domain; He stays when the missionary leaves. That is why the evacuation of the missionary is not necessarily catastrophic.

When the Italians occupied Ethiopia in 1935, they expelled all Protestant missionaries. In spite of the absence of the missionaries and persecution by the Italian authorities, the infant church grew by leaps and bounds between 1936 and 1942. Upon its return, the Hermannsburg Mission discovered that the Spirit of God had moved so mightily in the hearts of the Galla tribespeople that a mass movement to Christianity had taken place. In the southeast, the Sudan Interior Mission left 60 baptized believers in 3 small assemblies. Seven years later when the missionaries returned there were 18,000 believers in 155 churches!

When the missionaries were expelled from southern Sudan in 1964 they left behind a small struggling church still in its infancy. Persecution broke out. Pastors were killed and churches were burned. Some 250,000 refugees fled to nearby countries. During all this upheaval, revivals broke out and thousands of new converts registered their decision to follow Christ. In 1973 missionaries returned to engage in relief work.

Or take mainland China. The total evacuation of all missionaries, Roman Catholic and Protestant, was humanly speaking, an enormous loss, especially when many of their institutions and much of their property were taken over by the government. But China's loss was gain for other countries in that region of the world. More than 50 percent of the China missionaries were redeployed to other parts of the Far East and Southeast Asia. In 1950 there were only three missions in Thailand; today there are almost thirty. In 1950 there were only two missions in Taiwan; today there are over eighty. And the number of Protestant Christians in Taiwan has increased from 30,000 to 300,000. So God, who is able to make the wrath of man to praise Him, is able to deploy His servants in such a fashion that His purposes of grace for the nations are worked out. When one door closes, another opens. Happy is the missionary who is able to see the hand of God in the affairs of men and nations.

8. When doors are closed, they are not closed by man but by God. This is a daring statement, but it has the sanction of Scripture. In Revelation 3:7 Jesus Christ, the Head of the Church, refers to Himself as the One who "openeth, and no man shutteth; and shutteth, and no man openeth." The church has never had any problem with the first clause. That is God's business—to open doors. But what is this bit about closing doors? Does *God* close doors? Is that not the work of the devil?

During the fifth decade of the nineteenth century the church of Christ, like a mighty army with its banners flying, moved into China. On its banners were inscribed the words of Revelation 3:7, "[I am] He that openeth, and no man shutteth." It was a great day for the Christian church when its missionaries gained access to the most populous country in the world. Exactly one hundred years later the missionaries were again on the move, only this time they were coming out of China. The "mighty army" had been badly mauled; and the banners, tattered and torn, were trailing in the dust. But on those banners were inscribed the words of Holy Scripture: "[I am] He that . . . shutteth, and no man openeth" (Rev 3:7).

We rejoice and give praise to Almighty God when doors are opened. We say, "This is the Lord's doing and it is marvelous in our eyes." But when doors are closed we cry, "An enemy has done this."

According to Daniel 4:35 the most high God does "according to His will in the army of heaven, and among the inhabitants of the earth." It is not difficult to believe the first part about the army of heaven. But what about the inhabitants of the earth? Are they too under His direction and control?

What the church needs today is to take a fresh look at what the Scriptures have to say about the sovereignty of God. He knows the end from the beginning and is working all things after the counsel of His own will (Eph 1:11). He is able to make the wrath of man to praise Him (Ps 76:10). No man can stay His hand or say to Him, "What doest Thou?" (Dan 4:35).

If this is so, we can only believe that the door of China was closed by God, not by the devil. If it had not been God's will, all the armies of Red China could not have expelled the missionaries. But someone will say: "This is hard to believe and harder still to understand." It is difficult to understand; but we are not expected to understand everything God does. He has warned us that His ways are not our ways, nor His thoughts our thoughts. As the heavens are higher than the earth, so are His ways higher than our ways and His thoughts than our thoughts (Is 55:8-9). Paul reminds us that His judgments are unsearchable and His ways past finding out (Ro 11:33).

Anybody can believe in the sovereignty of God when the situation is under control; but when things get out of hand, when right is on the scaffold and wrong is on the throne, it is then that the Christian must take his stand on the Word of God and believe that in some mysterious way which we cannot fully understand, the purposes of God are being worked out according to His plan. He knows what He is doing even if we do not.

9. There are more open doors in the world than we can take advantage of with our present manpower. The real tragedy is not the number of closed doors that we can't enter, but the number of open doors that we don't enter. Instead of beating our breasts over the closed countries of the world, we should be recruiting men and women in ever increasing numbers to enter the lands that are open and ready to receive both the missionary and his message. Several facts should be borne in mind. The open countries far outnumber the closed countries. The opportunities in the open countries are greater than ever before. In many parts of the mission field people are turning to Christ in unprecedented numbers.

This is no time for retrenchment, much less retreat. The doors *are* open. The fields *are* white. The laborers *are* few. It is both foolish and futile to spend our time lamenting the few doors that are closed while we refuse to enter the many doors that are open. The closed doors are God's responsibility. We can safely leave them with Him. The open doors are our responsibility, and we neglect them at our peril.

10. There are no countries which are completely closed. A country is not necessarily closed simply because American mis-

sionaries are excluded. If all professional missionaries were to be excluded from a given country, it might still be possible for the nonprofessional missionary to enter. We must be more flexible at this point. Paul spoke of becoming all things to all men that by all means he might win some. There is no reason why Christian laymen should not live and work abroad for the purpose of bringing the gospel to countries closed to the professional missionary, especially in these days when the missionary corps is outnumbered by other groups, such as businessmen, military personnel, and government employees. Christian professors can teach and Christian students can study at Hindu, Muslim, and secular universities. In fact they have opportunities not usually afforded the average missionary.

And what shall be said about the ability of radio to penetrate the thickest curtain? Powerful missionary radio stations located in Quito, Addis Ababa, Monrovia, Monte Carlo, Manila, Seoul, Cheju, Bonaire, and the Seychelles Islands are beaming the Christian message in hundreds of languages into every corner of the habitable globe. There may be one or two countries without a Christian church, but there is none without a Christian witness.